Stories of Chinese Insect Pets

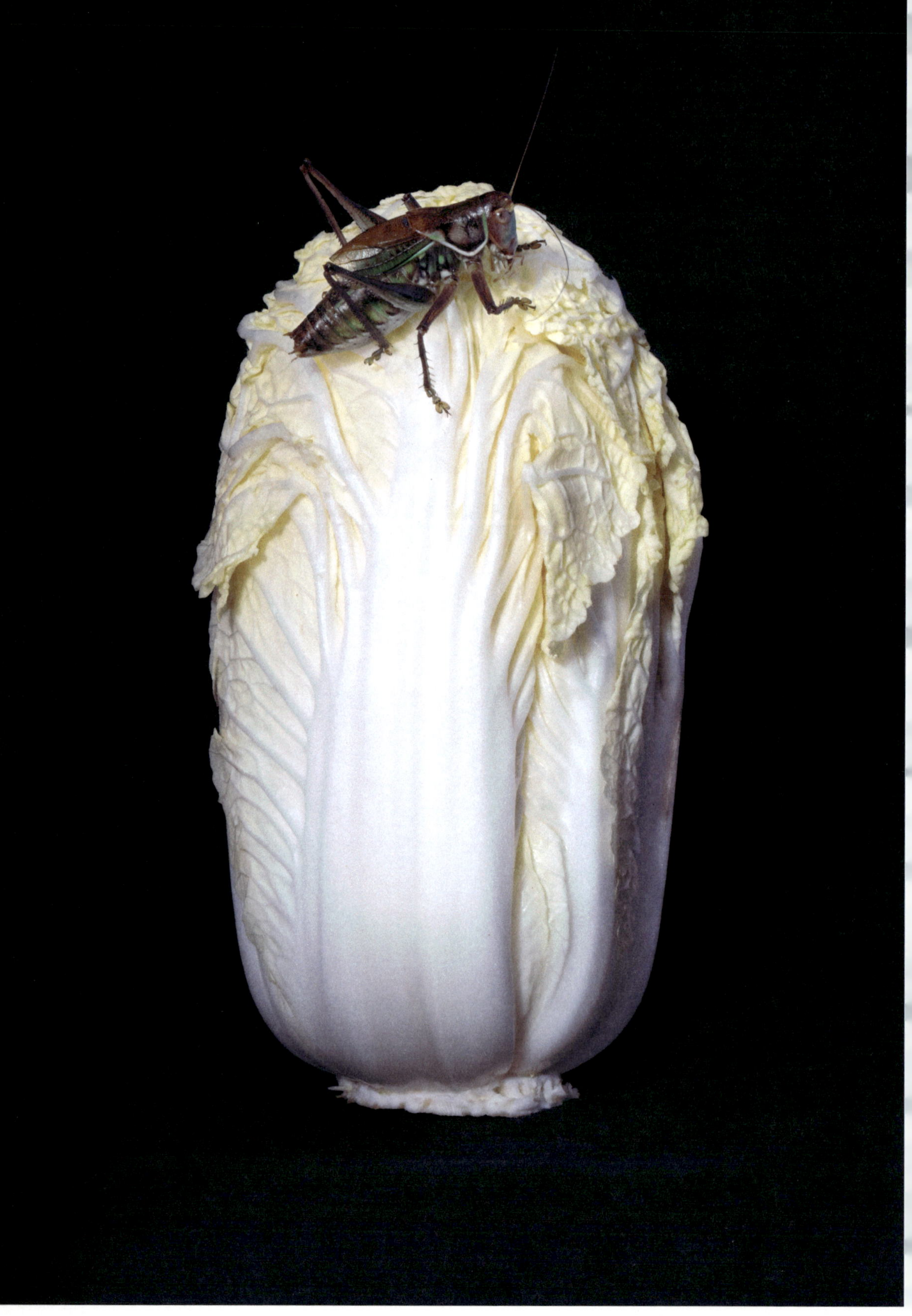

among other buyers, who want to get their hands on the future champion themselves. Today, the best fighters are said to come from a region in Northeastern Shandong Province, where the local climate supposedly produces a particularly fierce breed. Eager to dig into the cricket culture, I travelled to the village of Sidian, nicknamed the "cricket capital". The few hotels in the region are filled with cricket buyers in summer and resonate night and day with the chirping of the insects. Crickets have become a major source of income for locals – one cricket recently sold for 50,000 yuan, or nearly 6,300 euros. Skyrocketing cricket prices are prompting numerous locals to take up cricket hunting, which is now said to provide 100 million yuan a year for the local economy, or about 12,5 million euros. Hunters take time off work for two months in summer, usually earning much more than their regular salary. In Sidian, I met the Lu family, who have been hunting crickets for several generations. Like most women in the region, the grandmother looks for crickets at sunrise, in the corn fields around her house. She then drives her moped to the local market to sell her catch to the traders who each rent a space with a small table on the sidewalk. When the sun sets, she goes back in the fields to find more. Men catch crickets in groups at night, sometimes after long hours of driving. The capture equipment is simple: a flashlight, a net and a container. With the Internet, the cricket hunter's work has evolved and the new generation tends to sell directly to customers. By recording videos showing the aggressiveness and combat skills of their catch, then posting them on social media, they reach buyers from all over the country and send the insects directly by mail. Many hunters complain about the decrease in number of insects harvested today and attribute this change to increasing pollution.

Cricket fights typically take place in small transparent acrylic arenas with a removable divider separating the two insects. Each owner stirs up the aggressiveness of his cricket by shaking a dry grass in front of his antennae. When both opponents seem excited enough, the separation is removed, and the fight can begin. A good fighter will open its mandibles wide and fiercely assault its opponent. After a few quick attacks, the loser will generally back off, while the winner emits loud victorious stridulations. The rules to judge matches have evolved little since their creation in the 13th century, and an elaborate system is used to categorize fight styles, with poetic names describing the different moves. In most cases, fights do not end up injuring the insects – although I have sometimes witnessed severed antennae and legs. Once a cricket has lost a fight, it is considered useless and released to roam free.

Today, crickets are undoubtedly more popular for fighting than singing. During my visit, I met mafia members who came chauffeur-driven to Sidian to buy million yuan's worth of crickets for fighting, or 125,000 euros. A week after my return to Switzerland, an article in the press announced a police raid in the middle of an illegal cricket fighting tournament in an outlying area of Shanghai. Although fighting is legal in China, gambling is not allowed. But all the aficionados I met admitted: cricket fights without bets are boring. – Laurence Kubski

Laurence Kubski

Crickets

Simonett & Baer

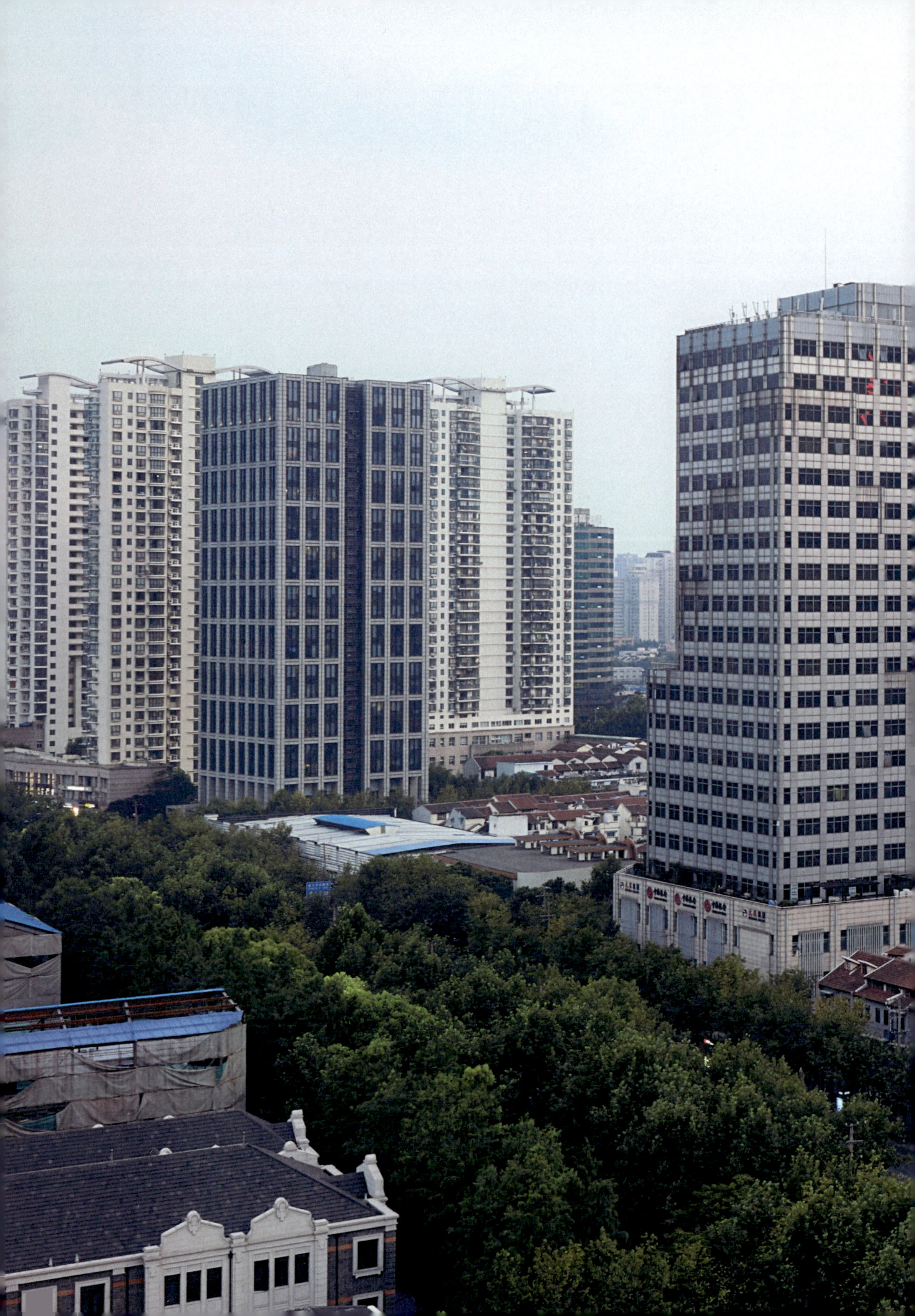

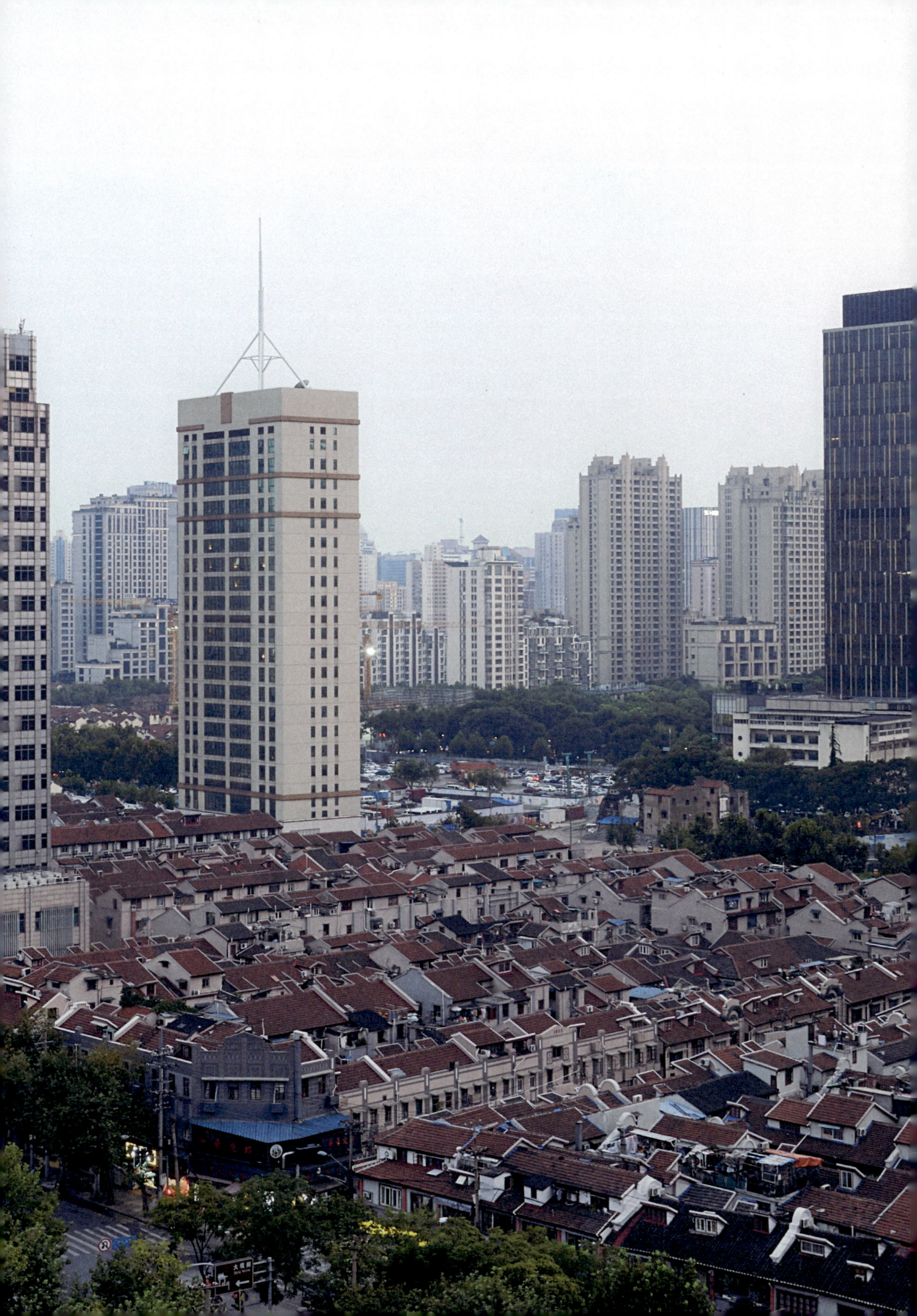

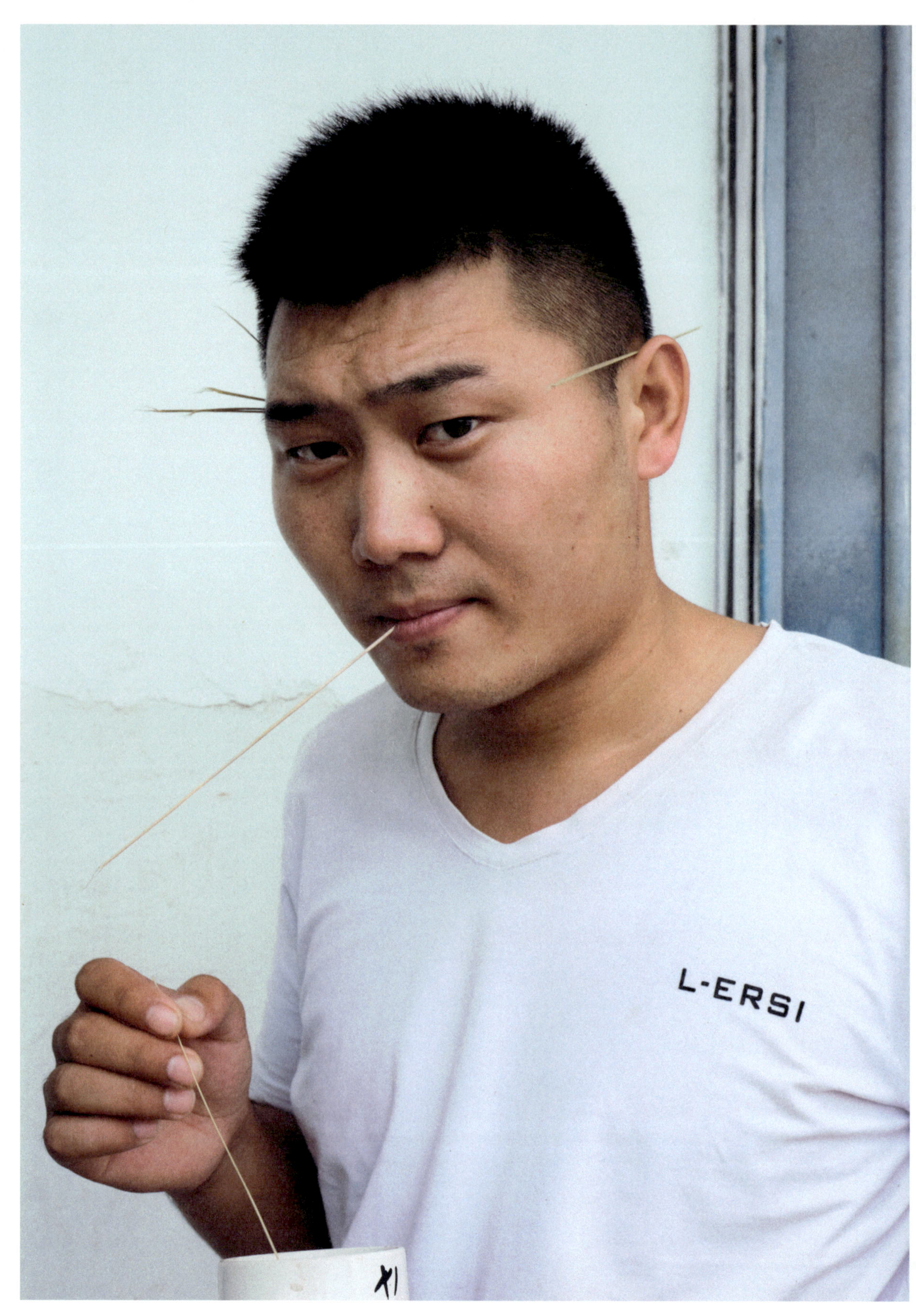
L-ERSI

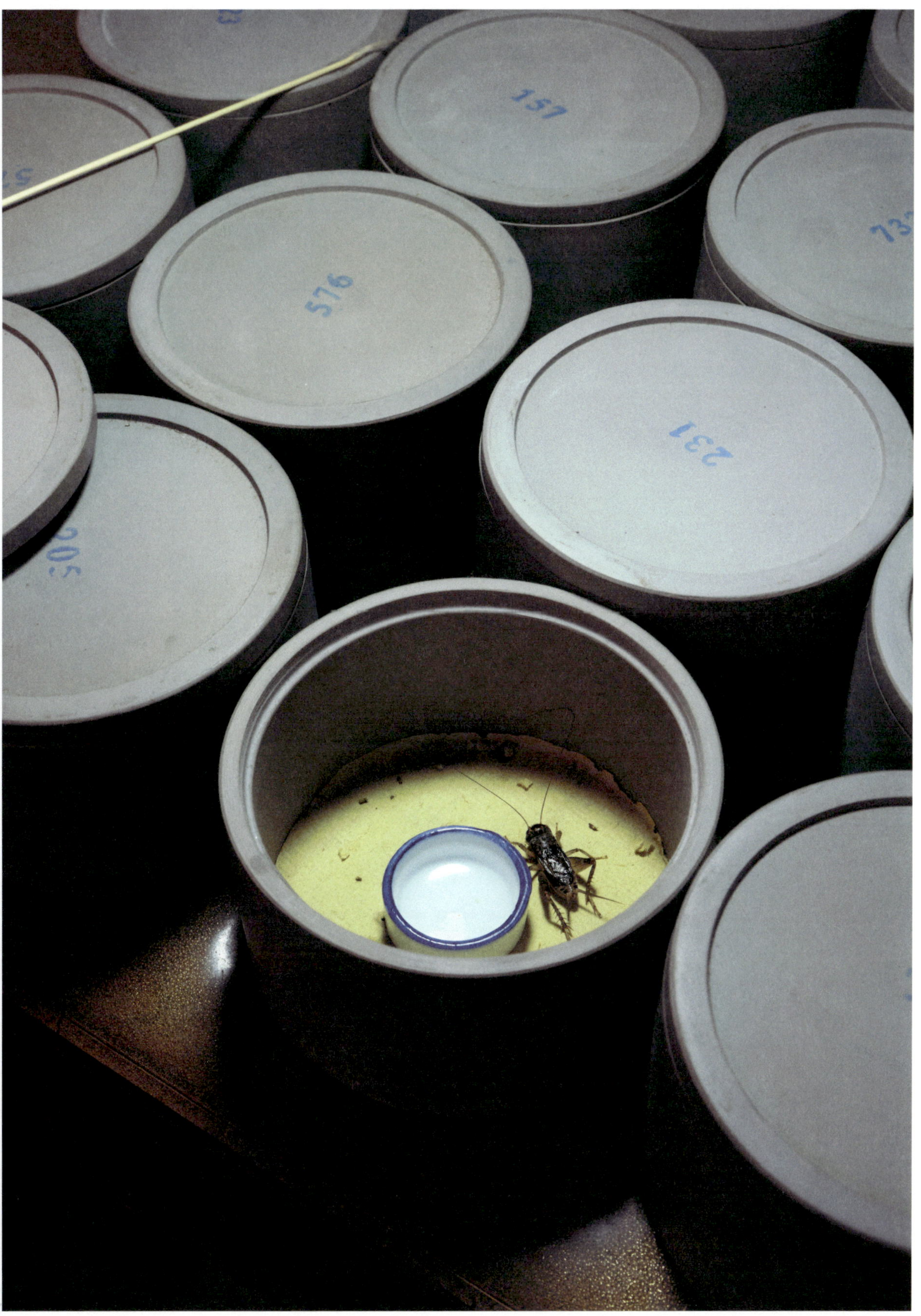
157
576
231

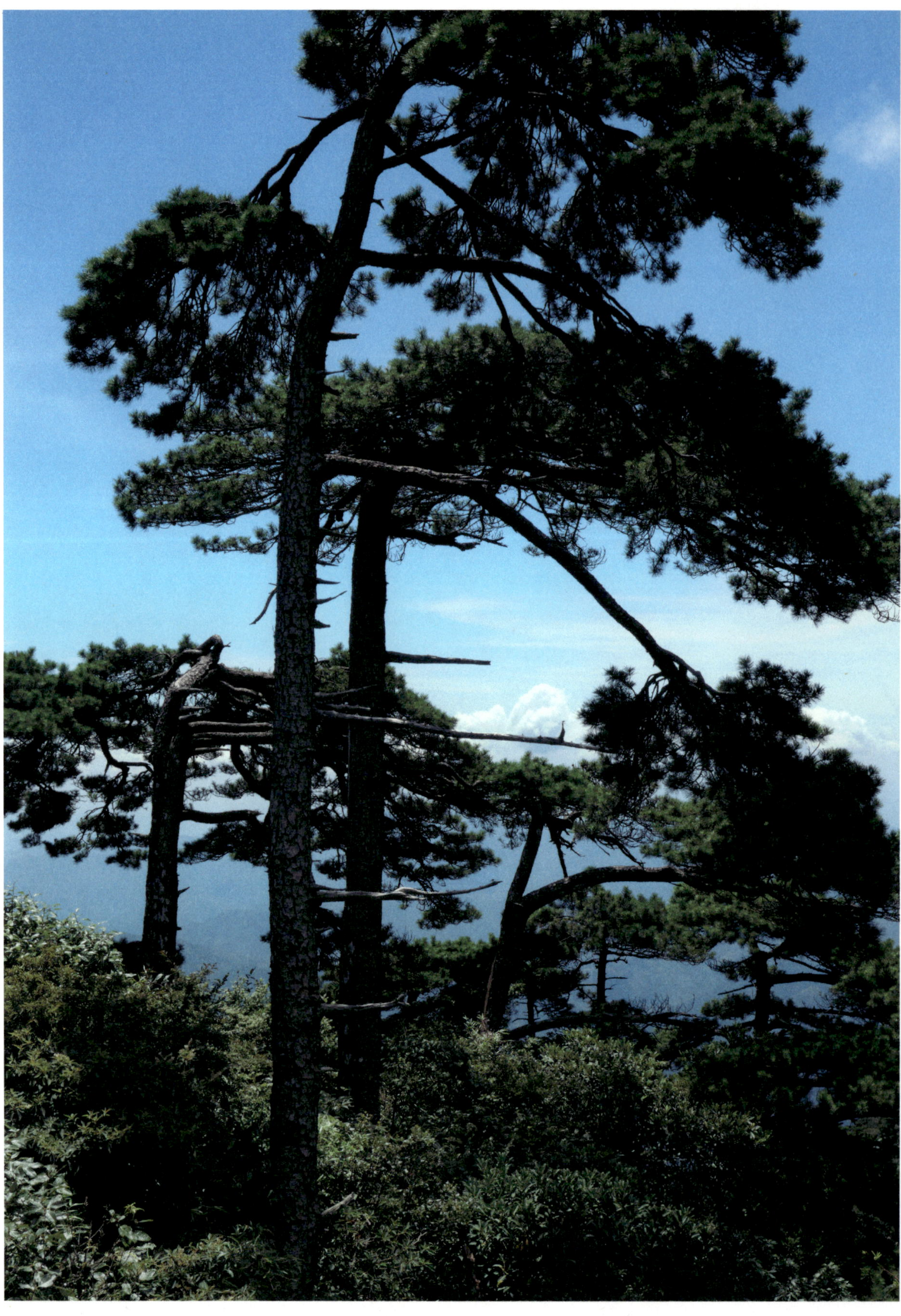

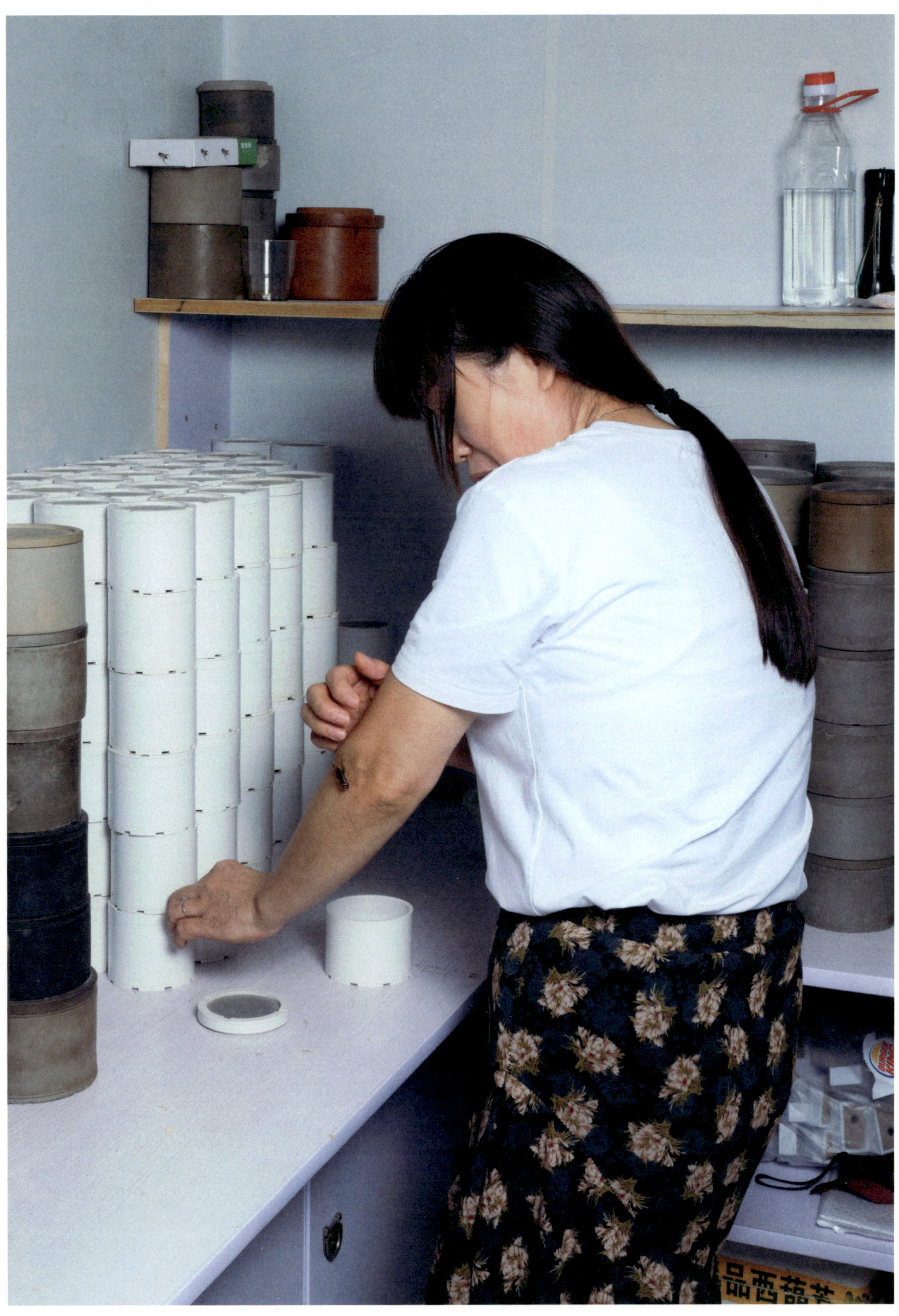
BURGER

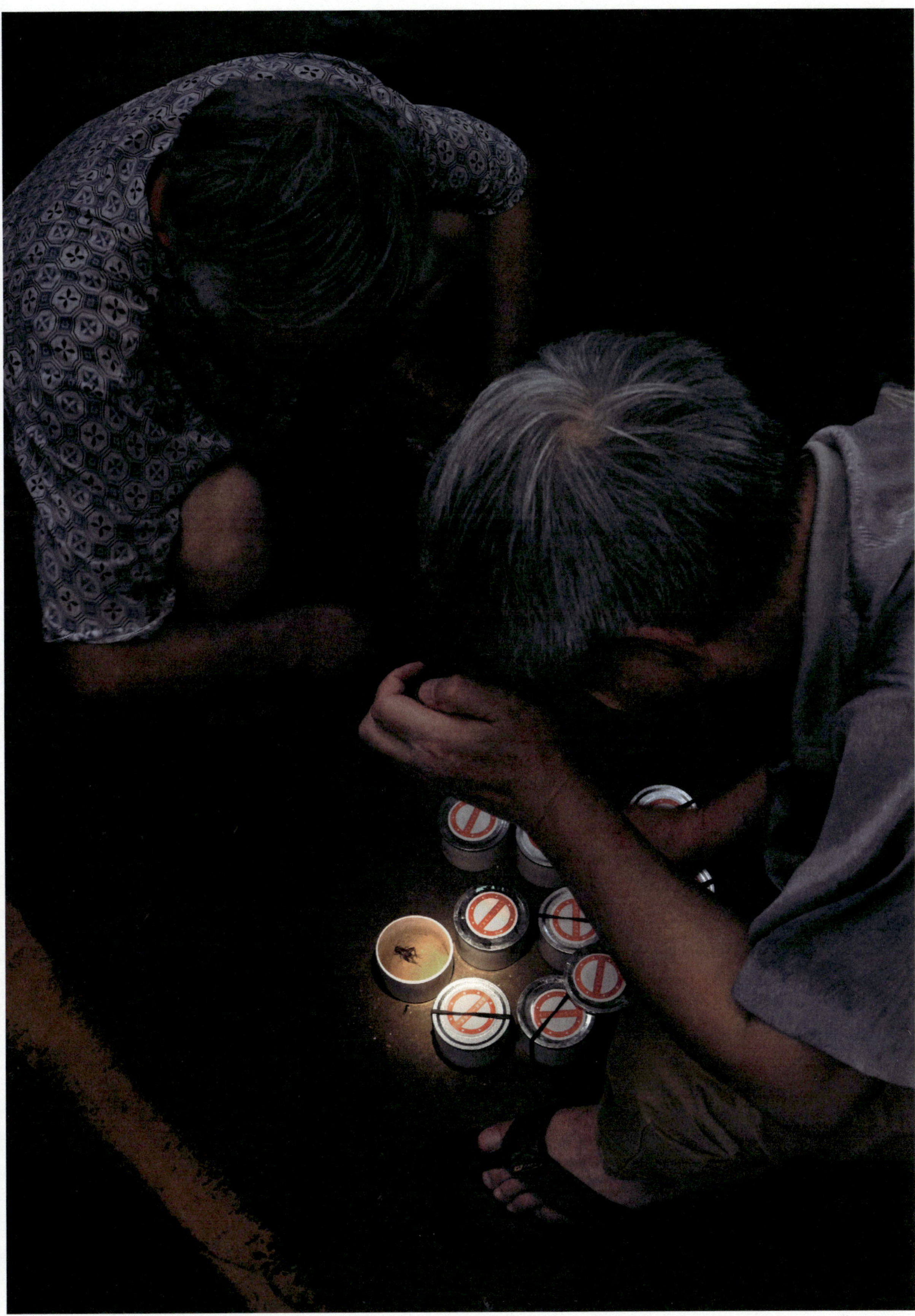

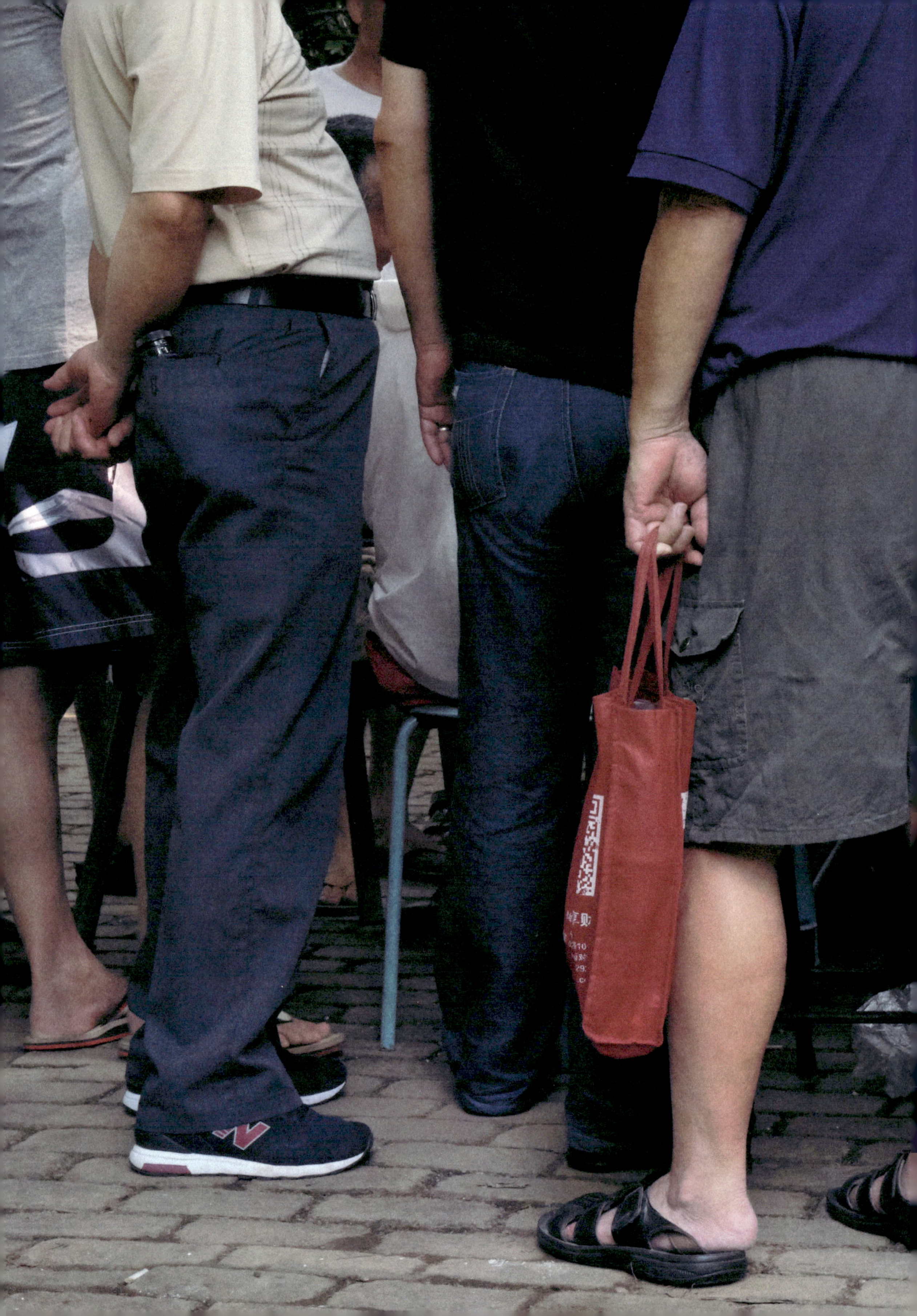

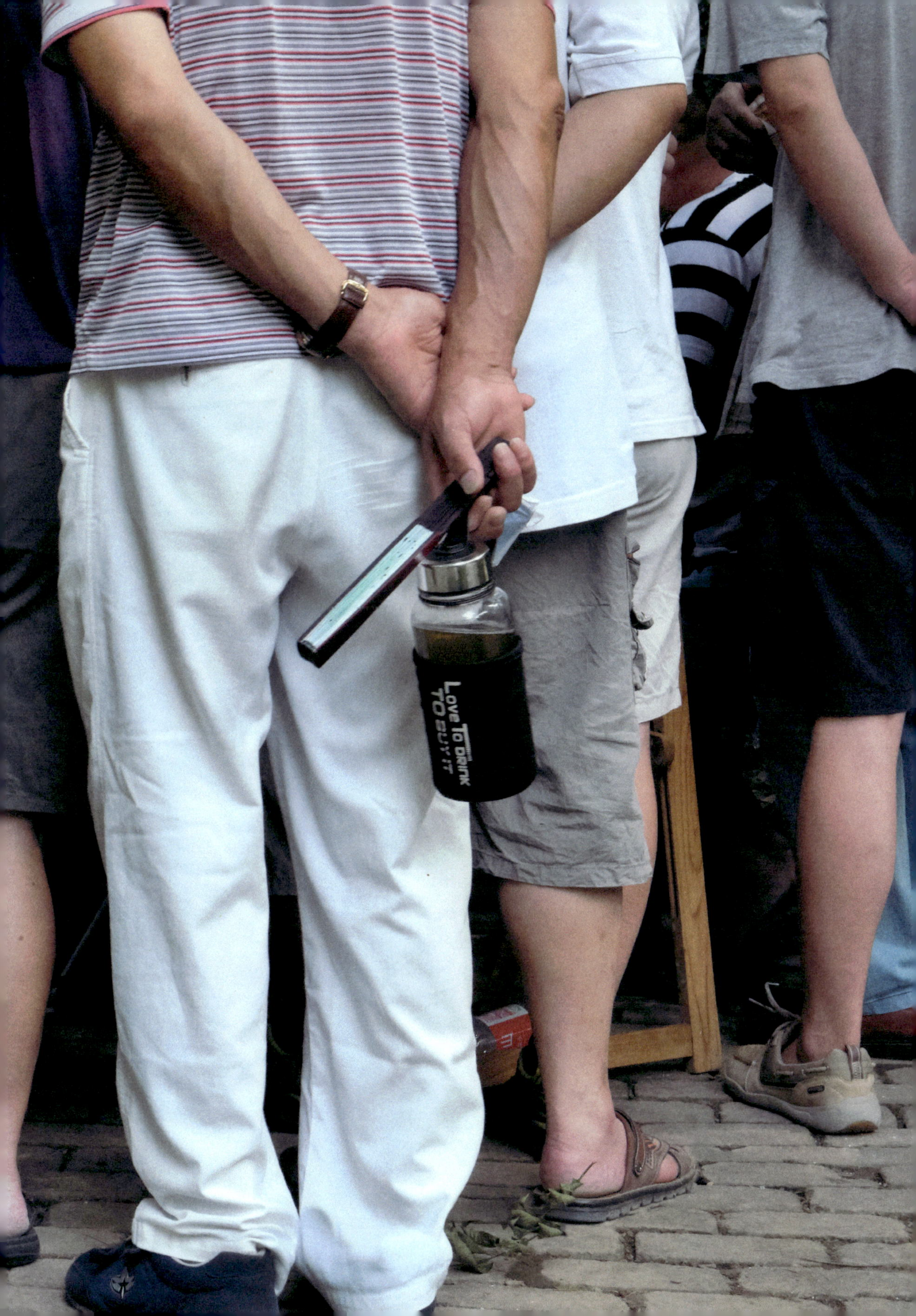
Love To DRINK
TO BUY IT

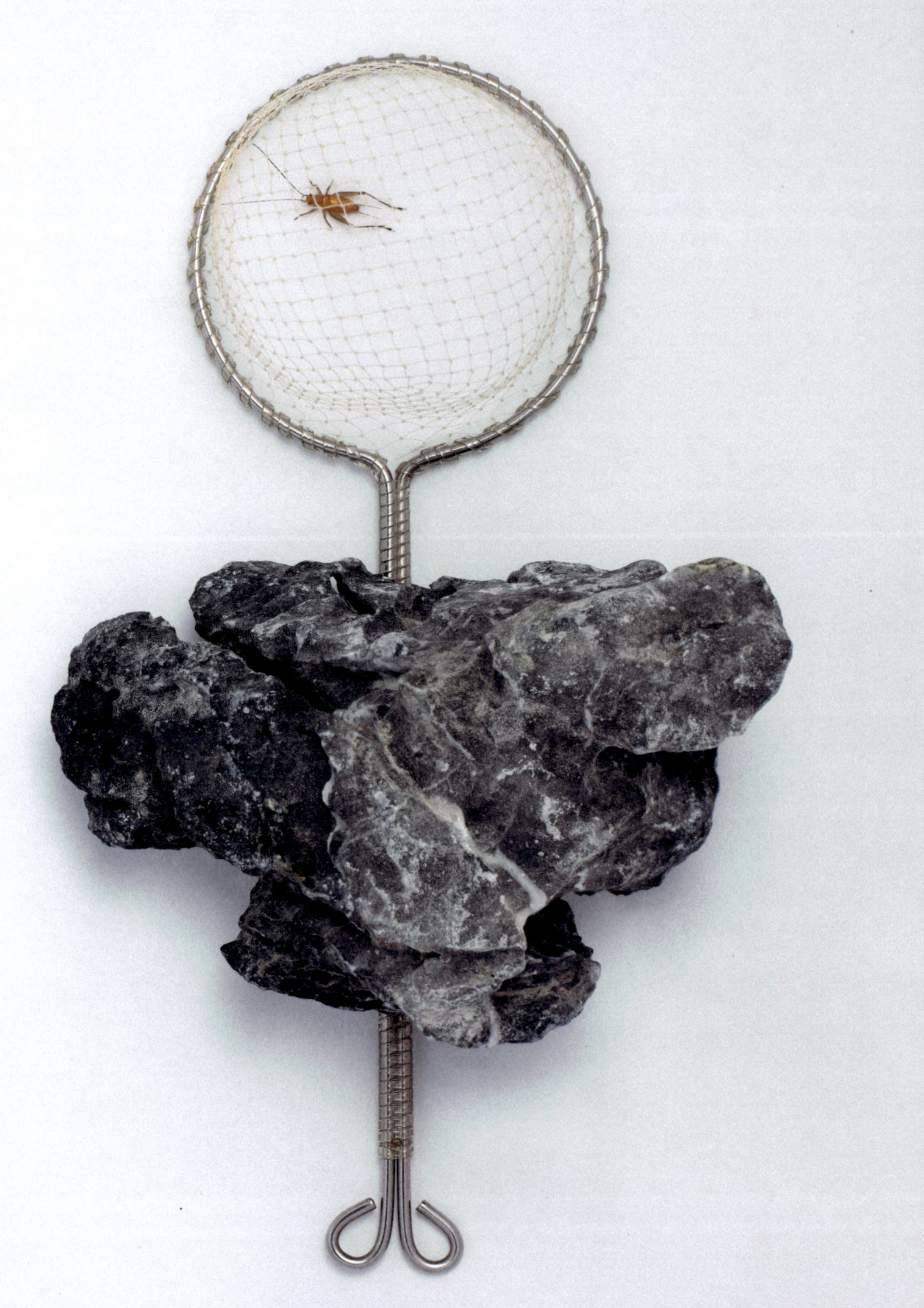

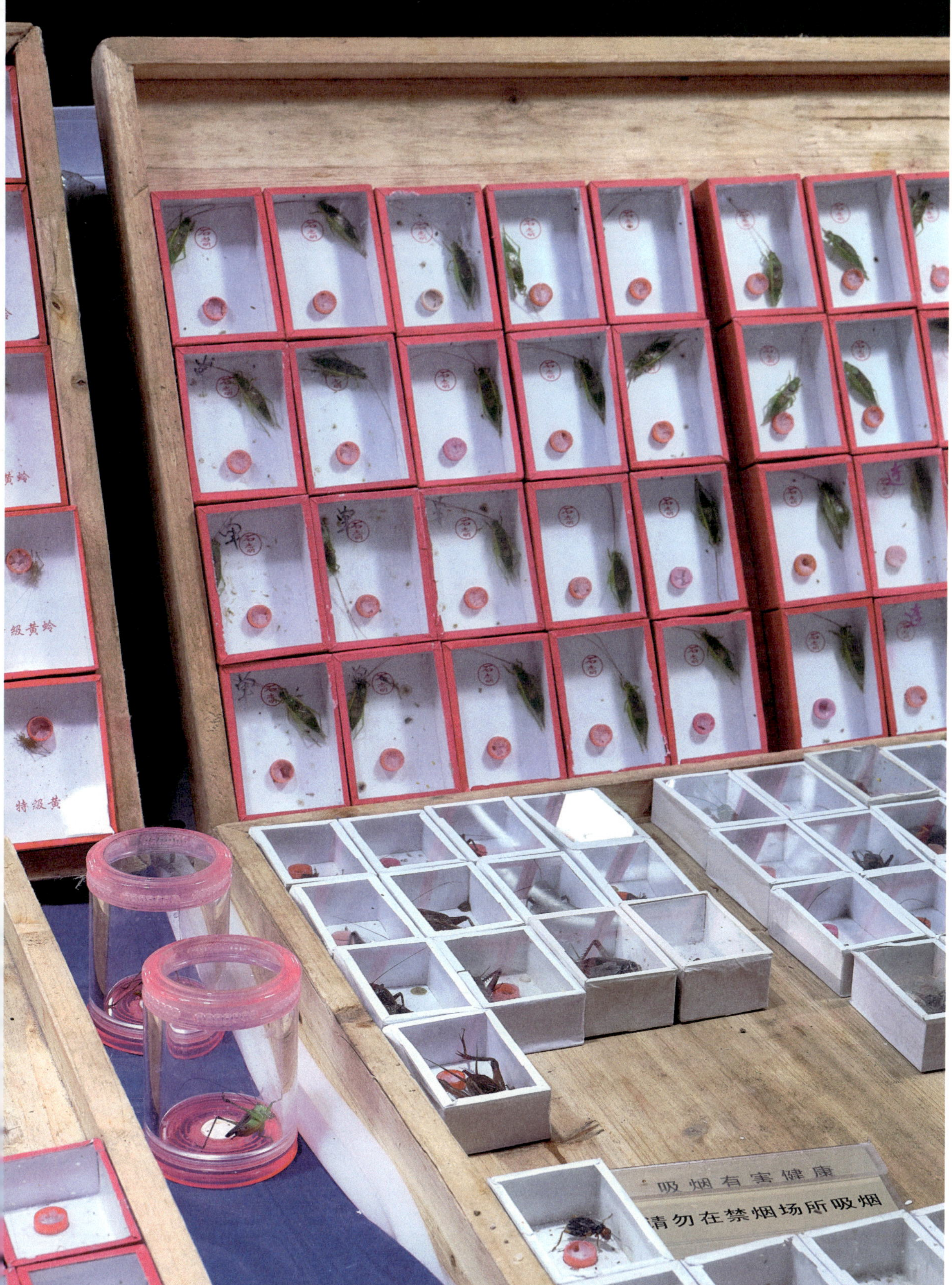
黄蛉
级黄蛉
特级黄
吸烟有害健康
请勿在禁烟场所吸烟

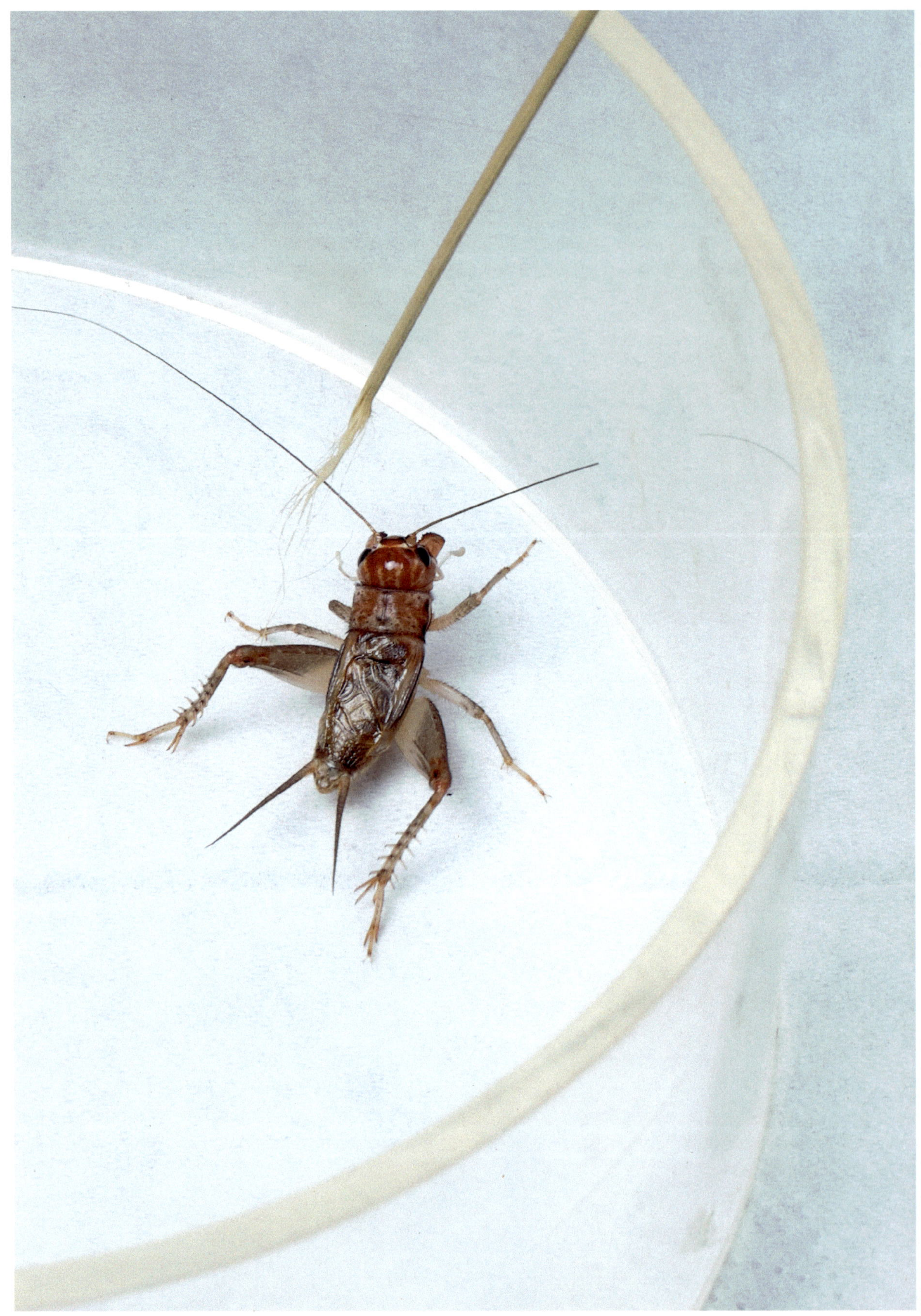

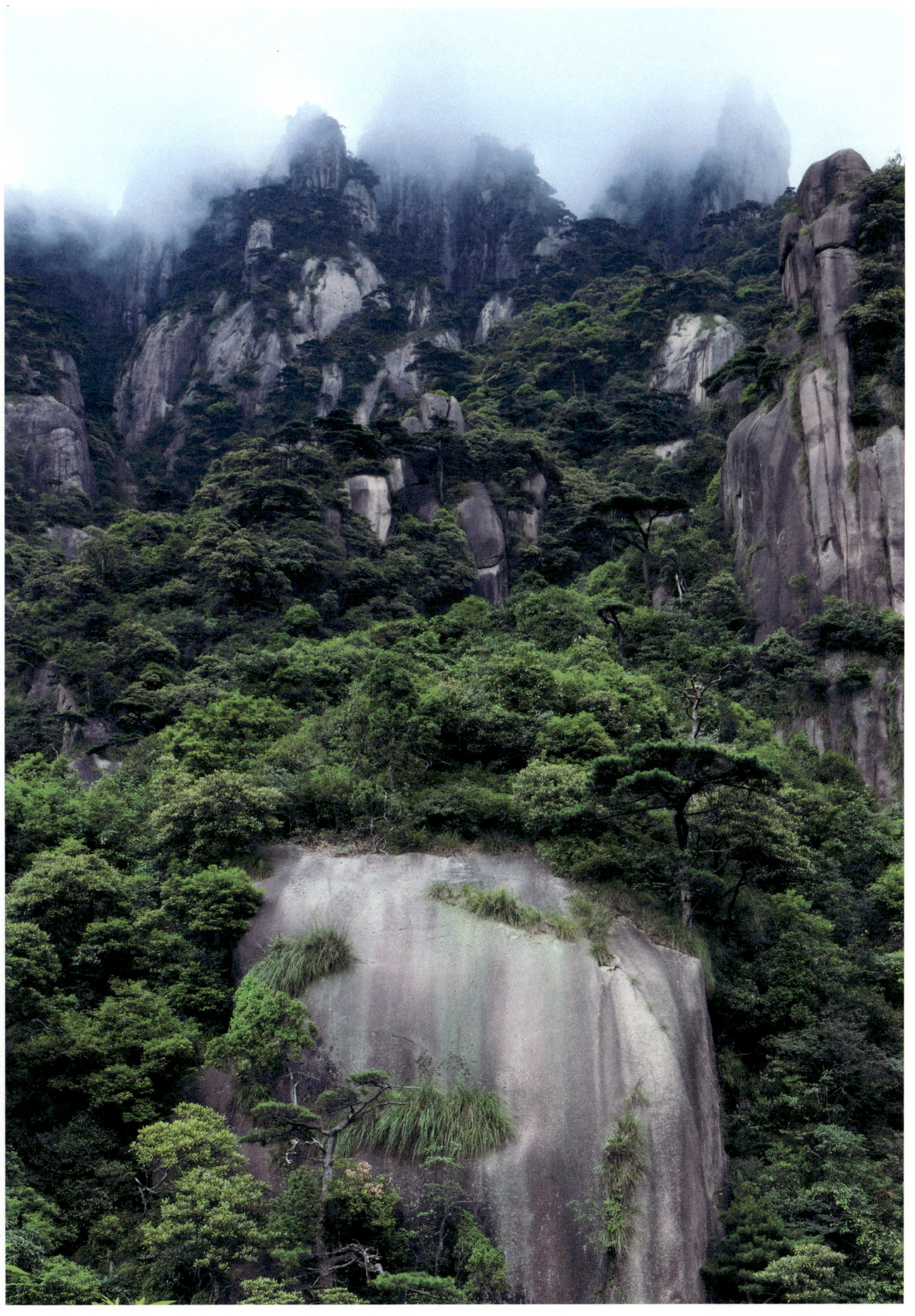

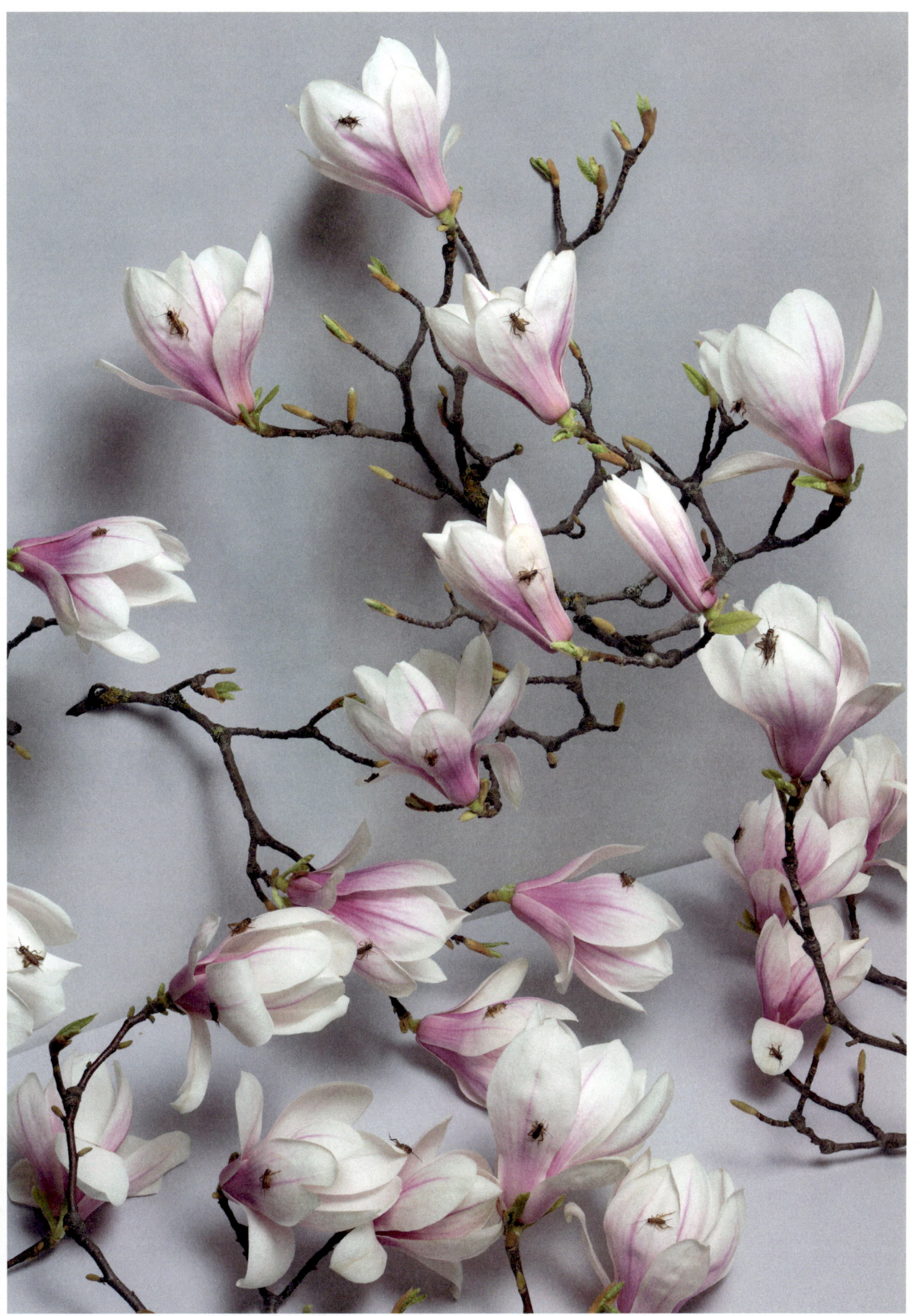

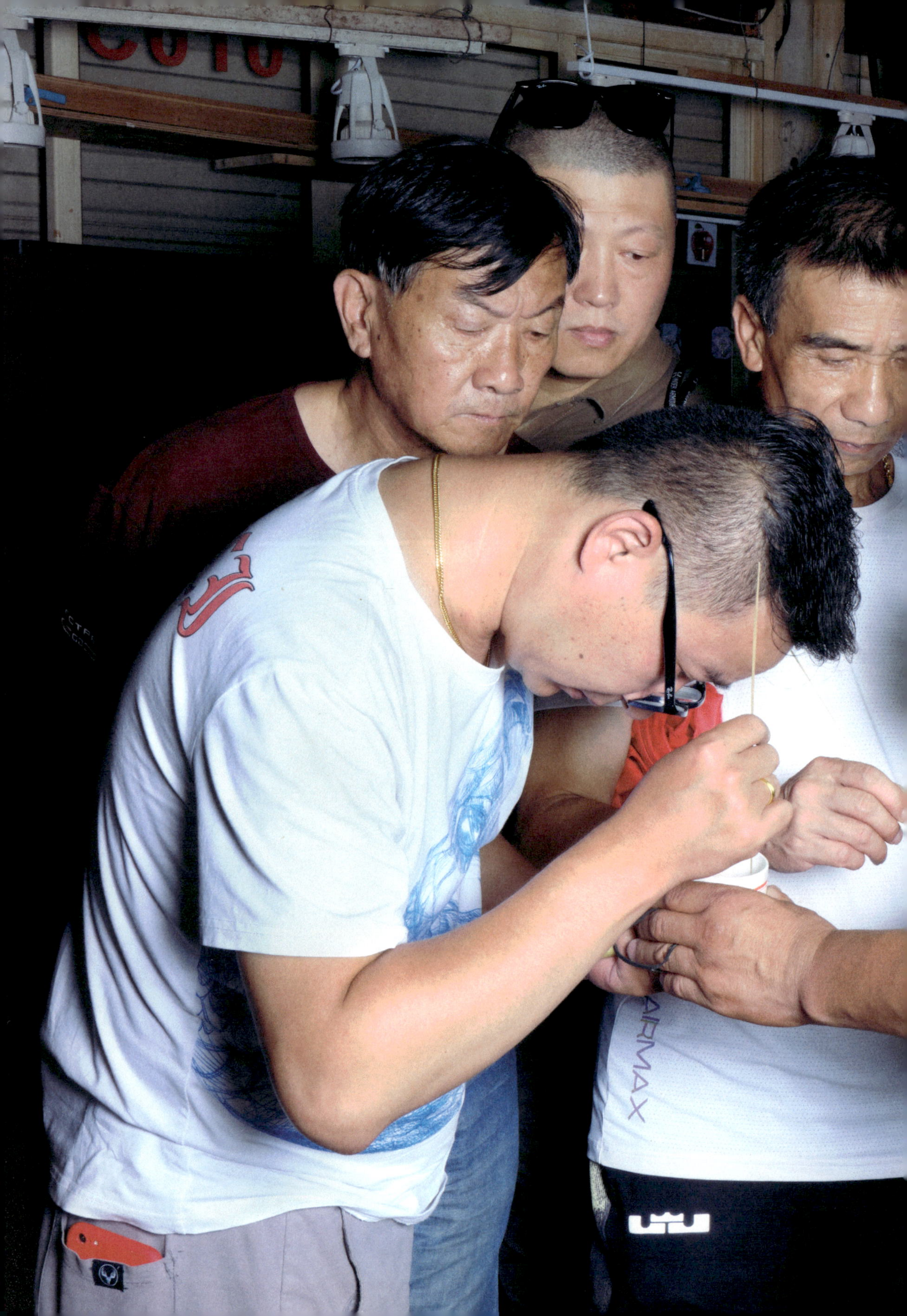
AIRMAX

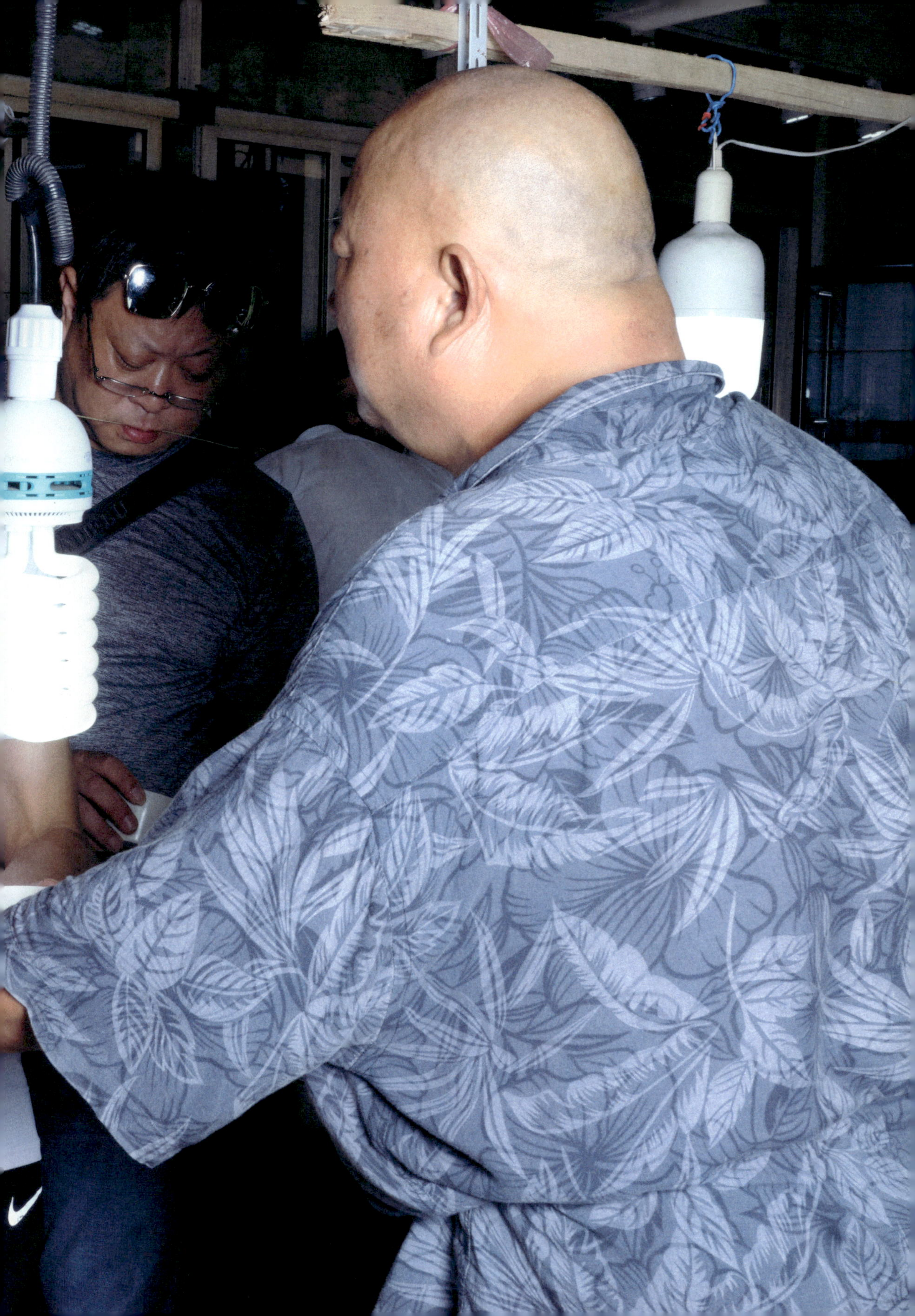

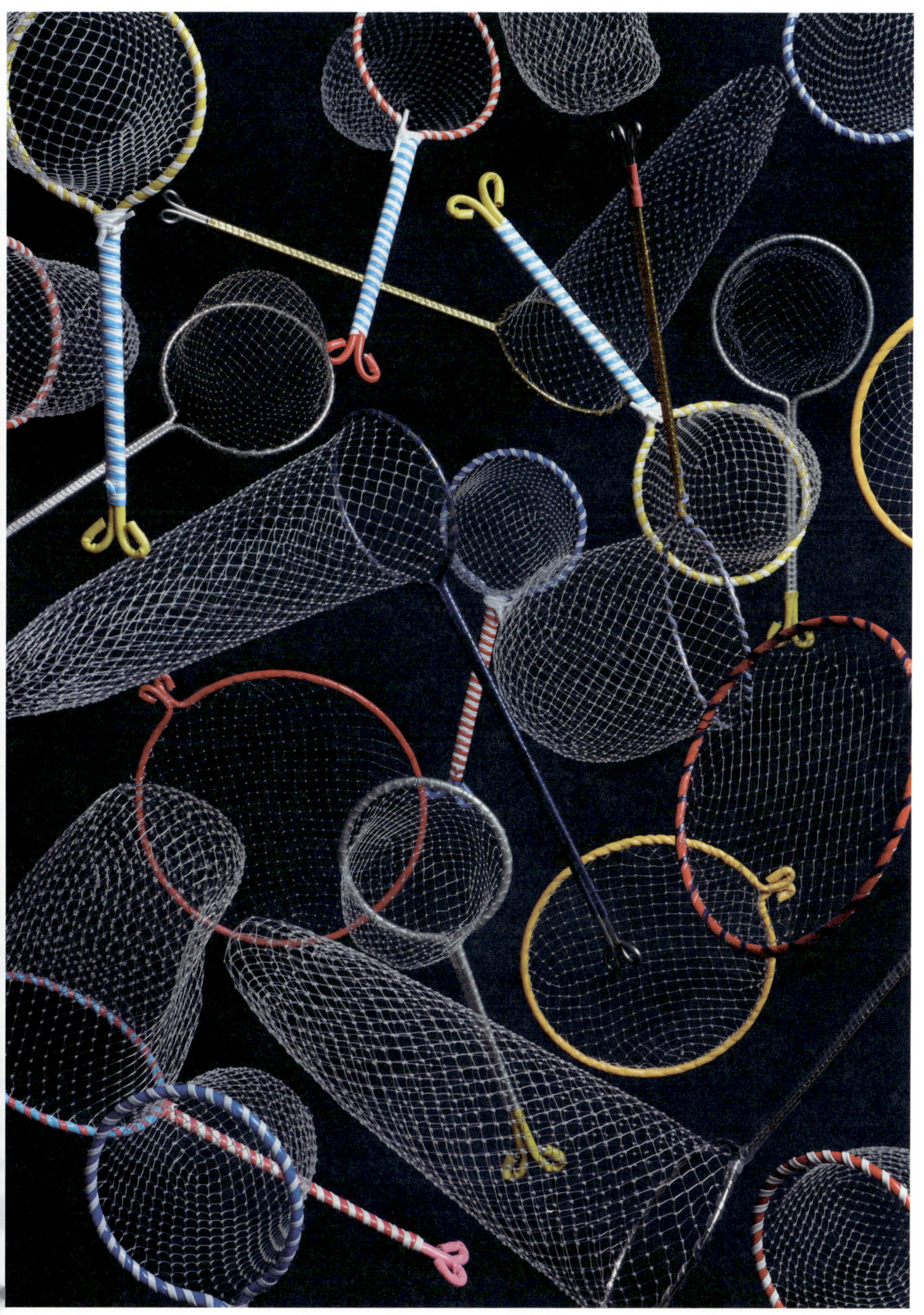

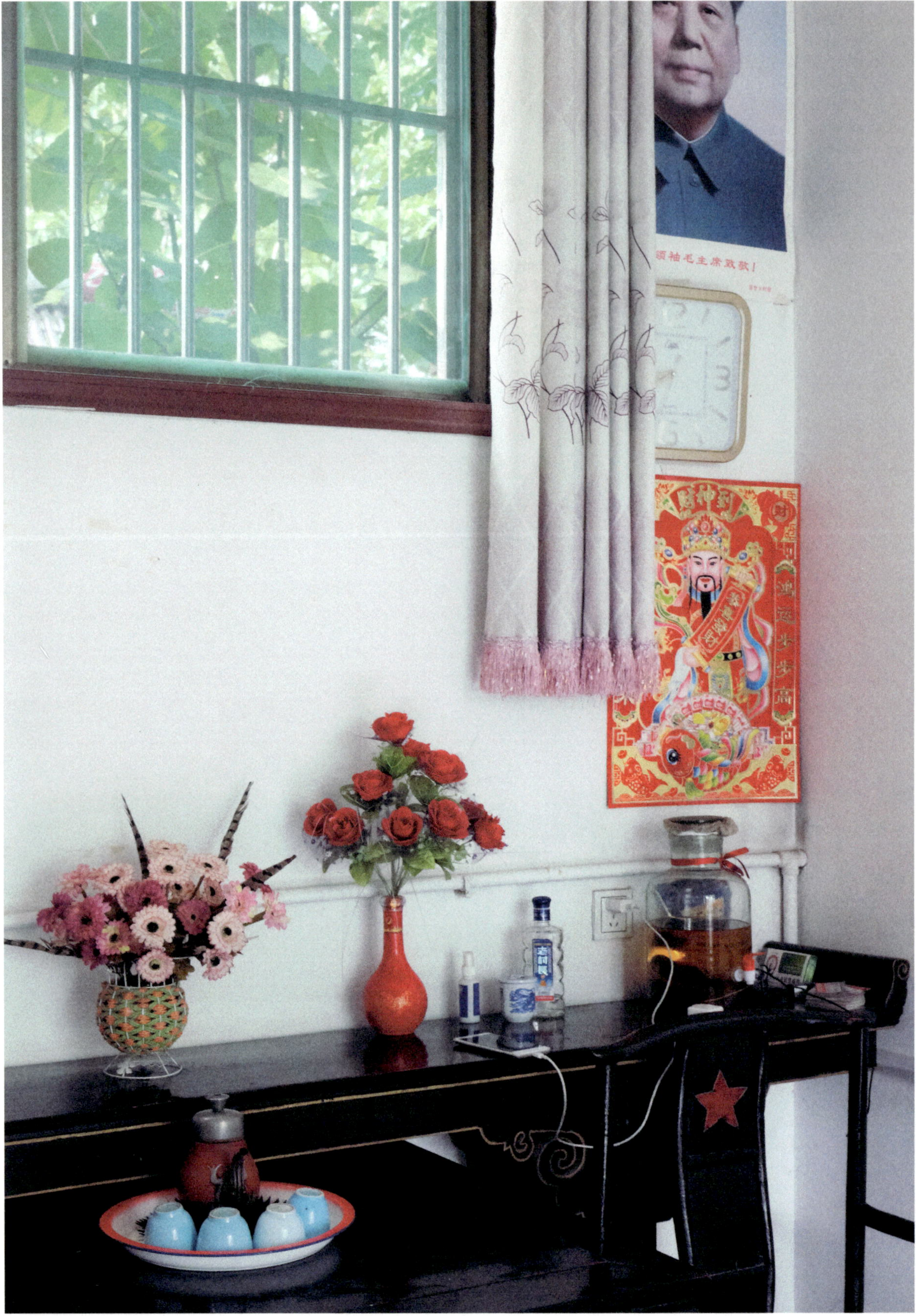
领袖毛主席致敬!
财神到
鸿运步步高

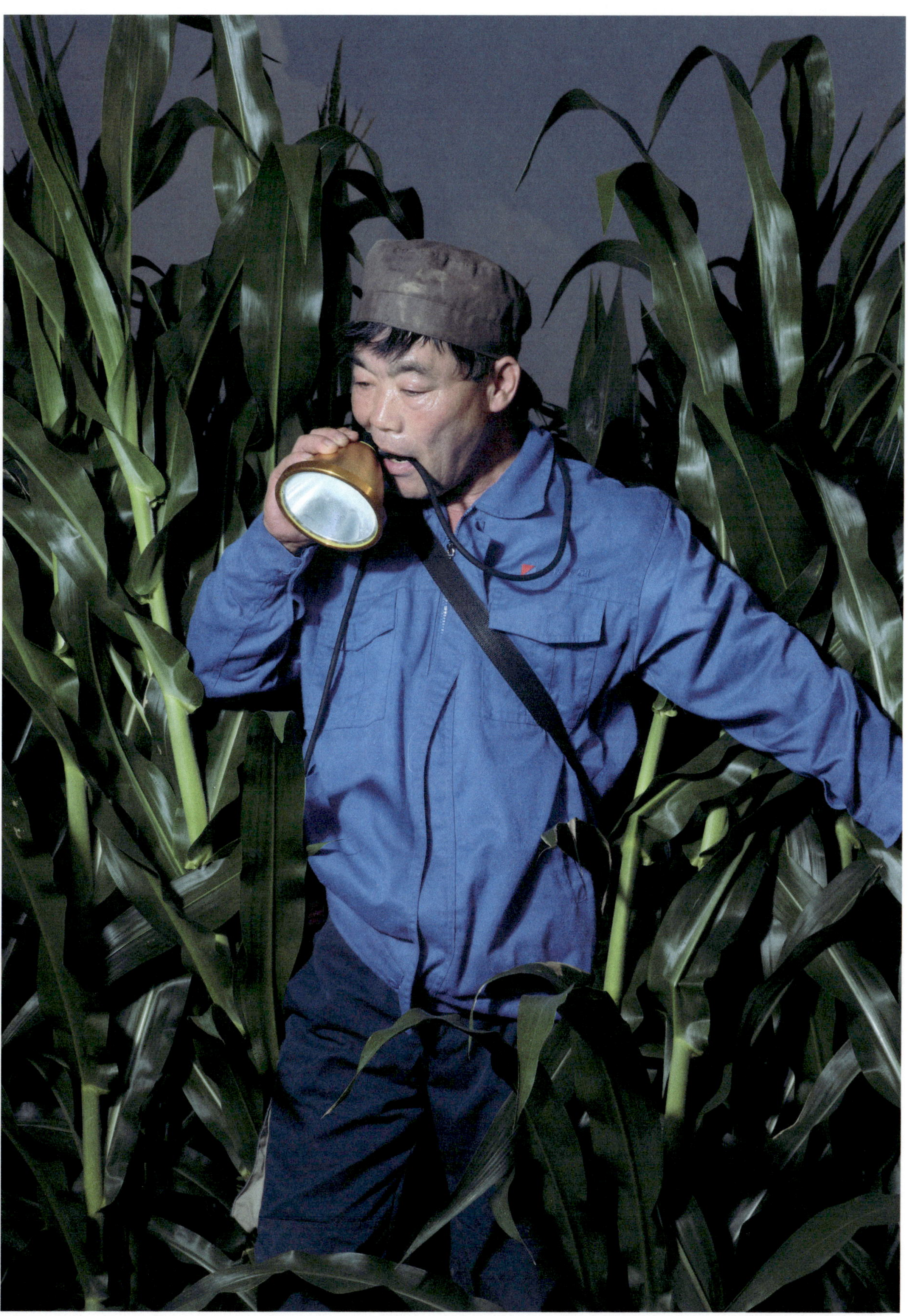

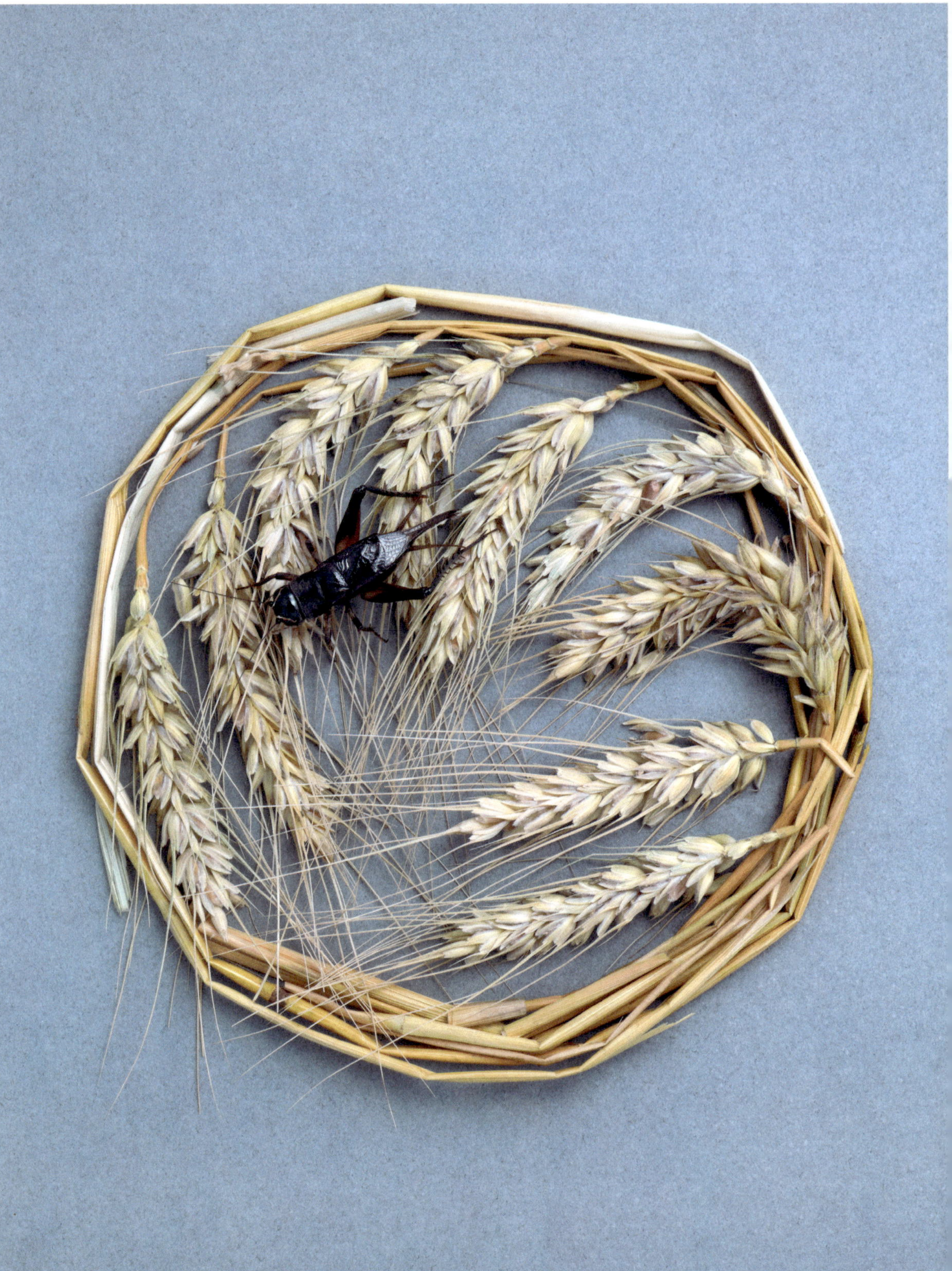

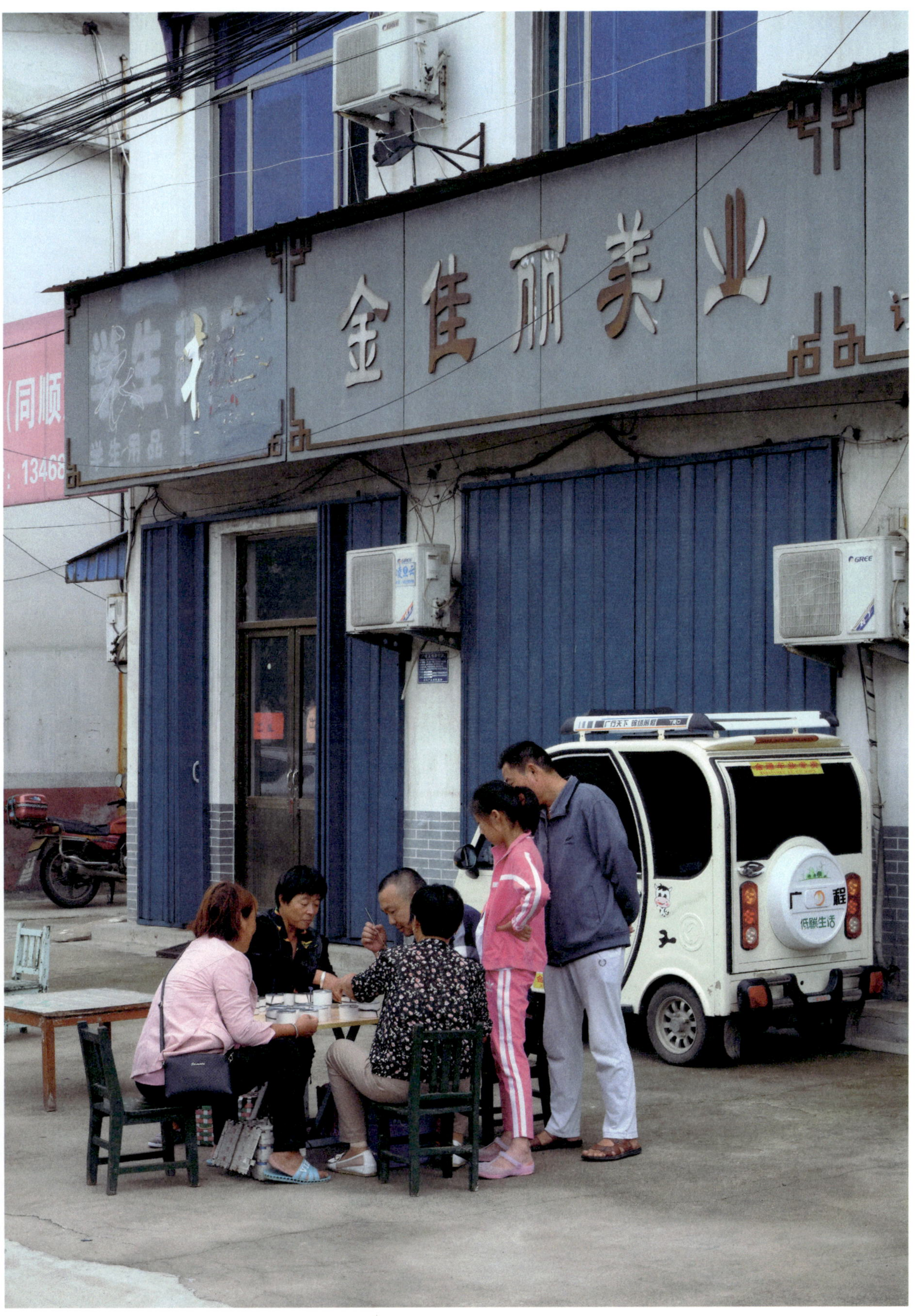
金佳丽美业
(同顺
13468
GREE

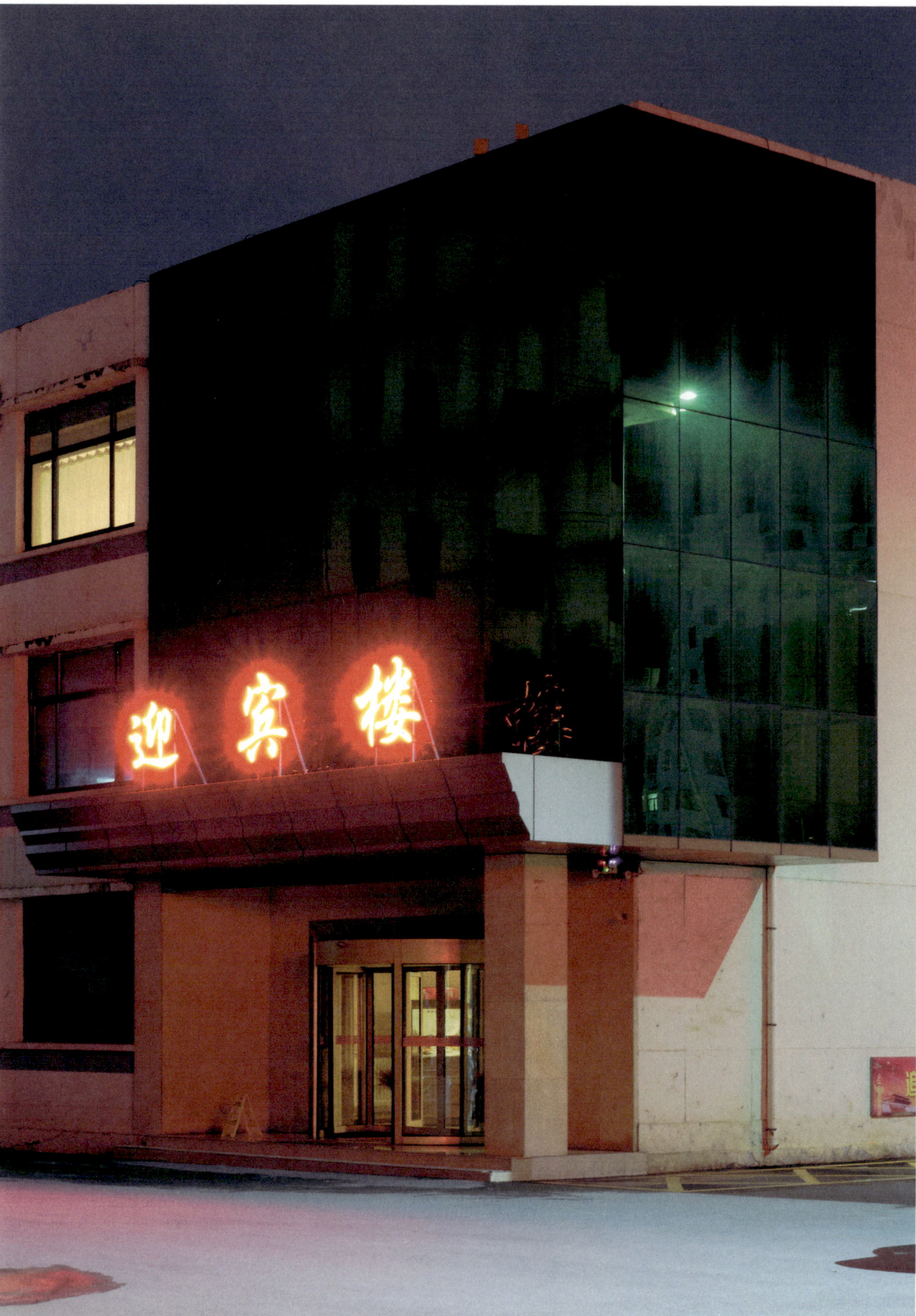
迎宾楼

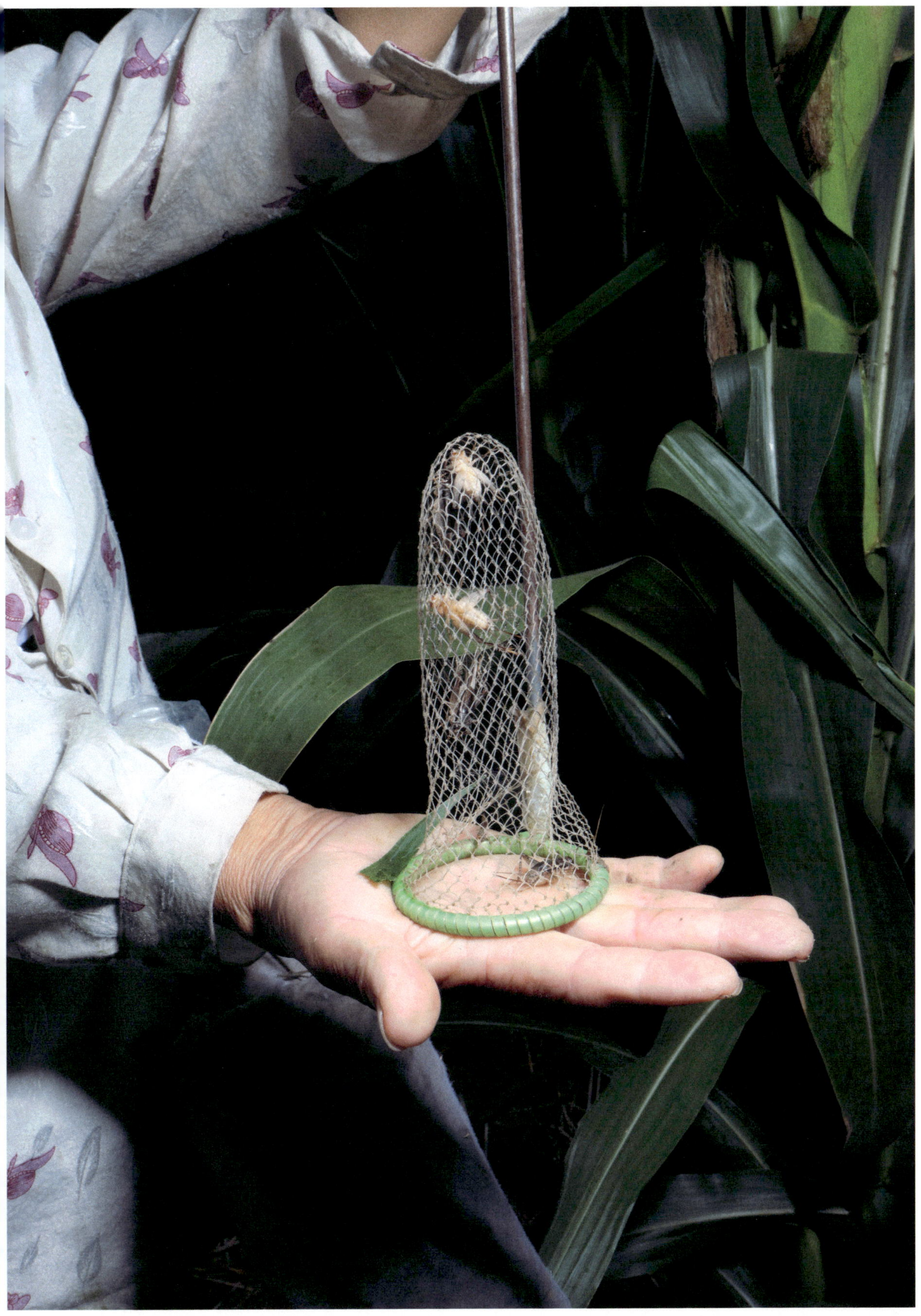

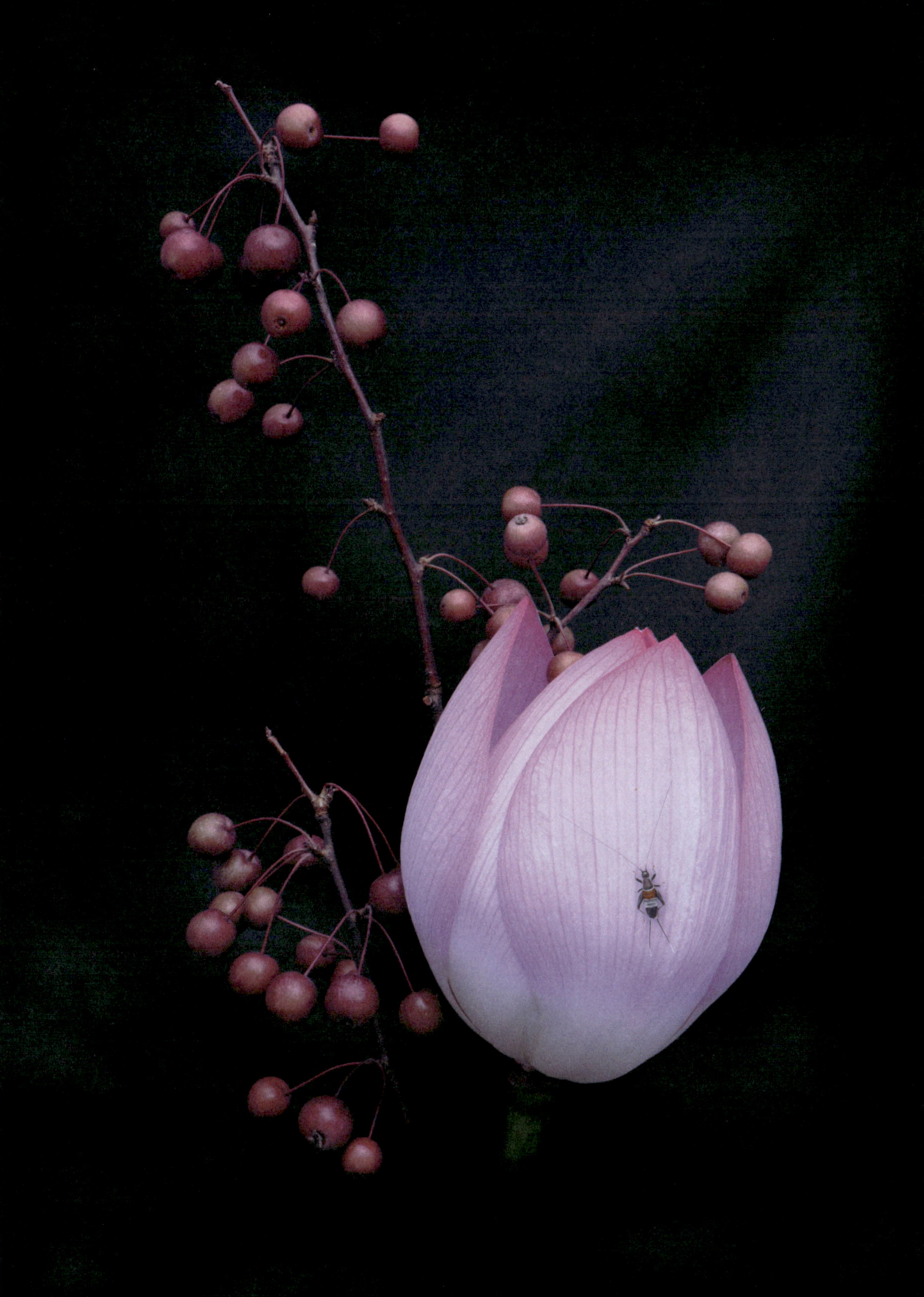

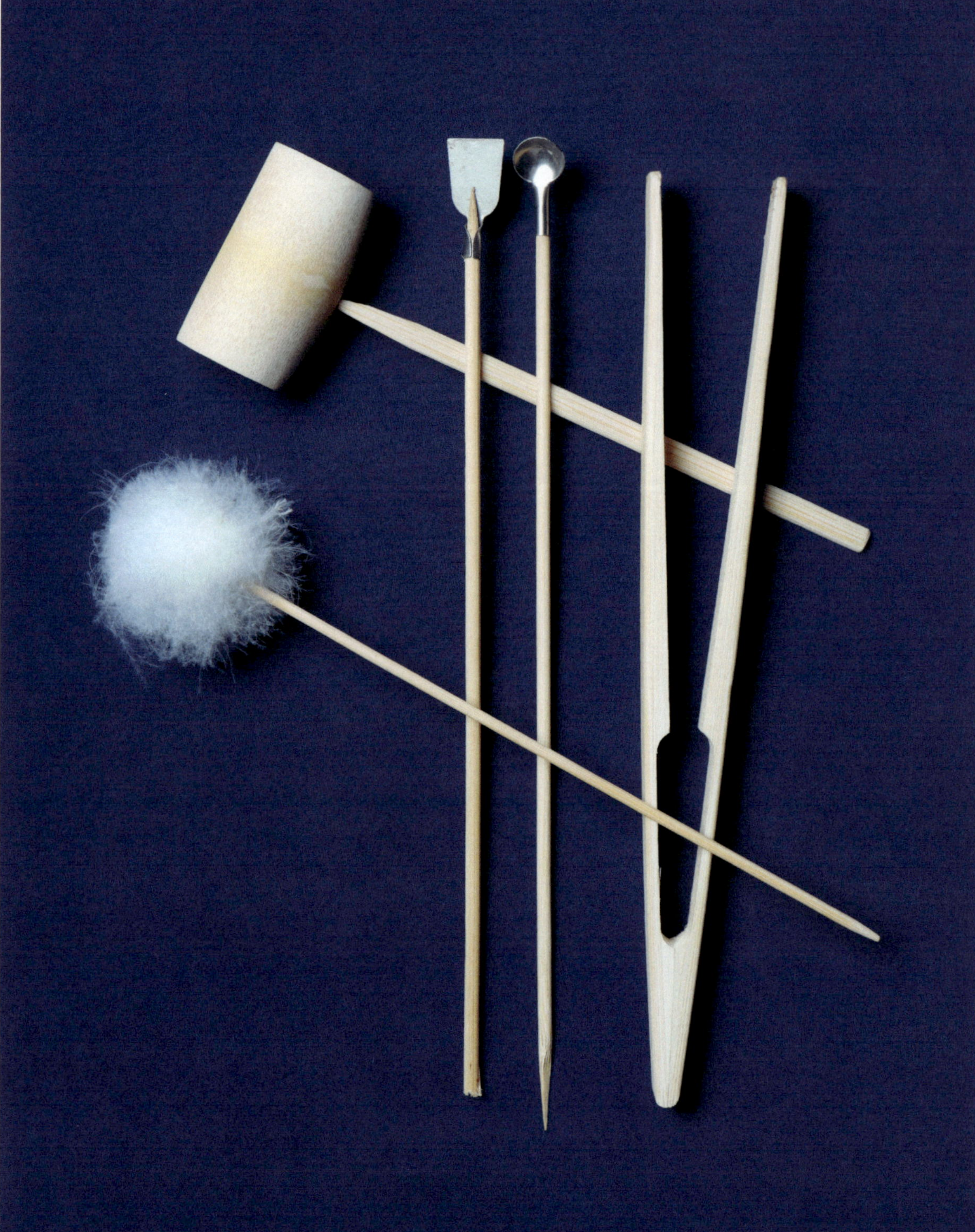

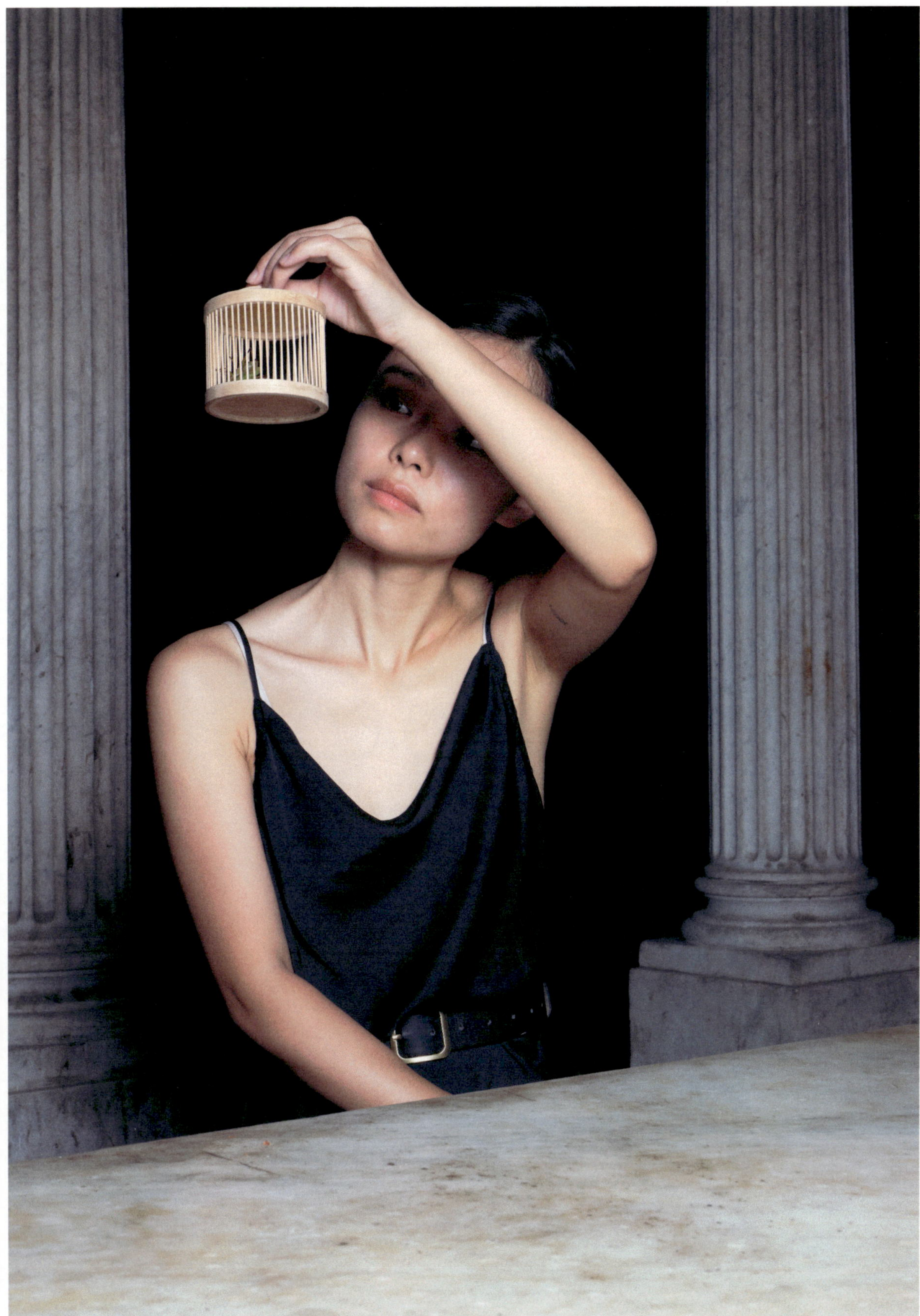

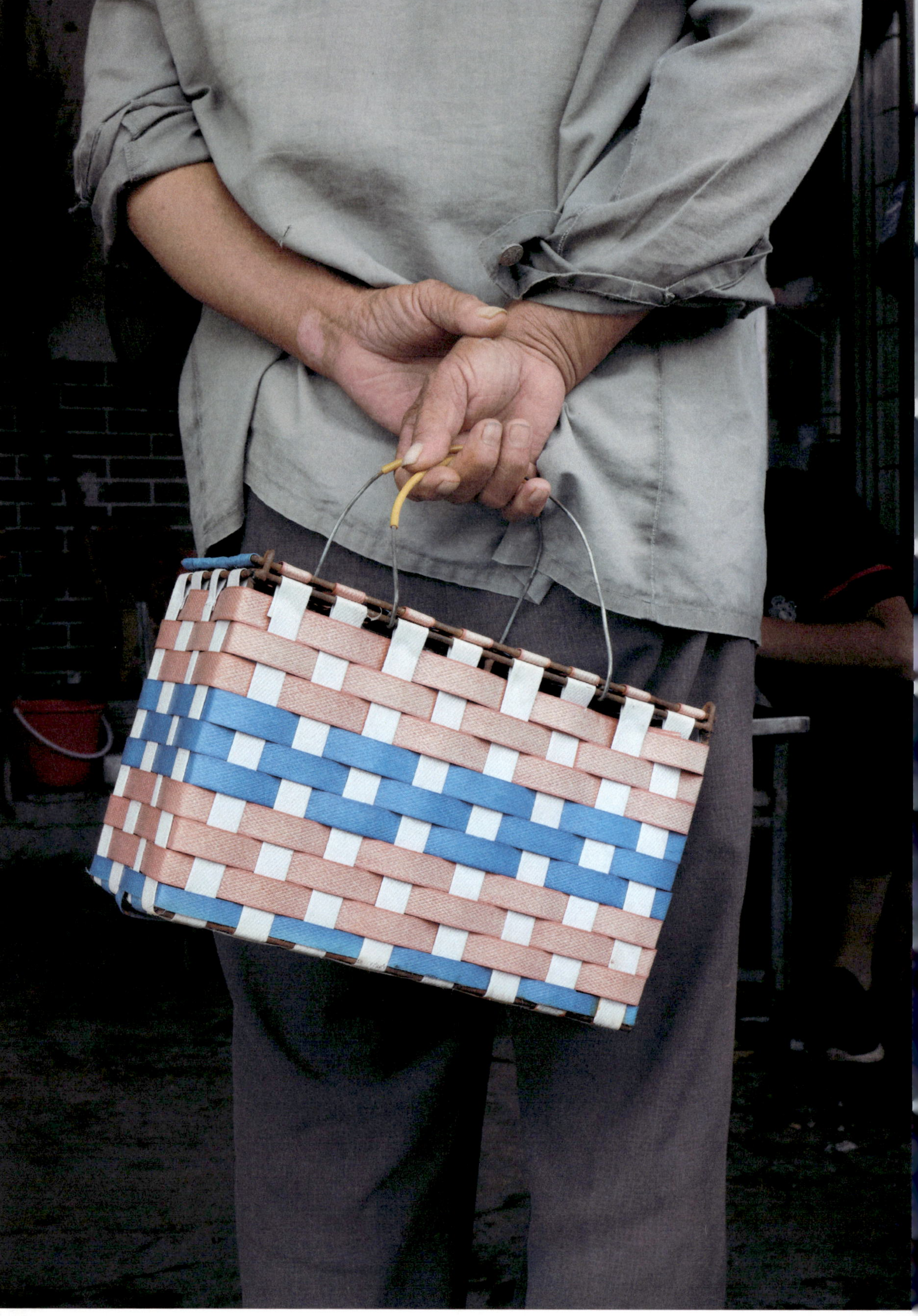

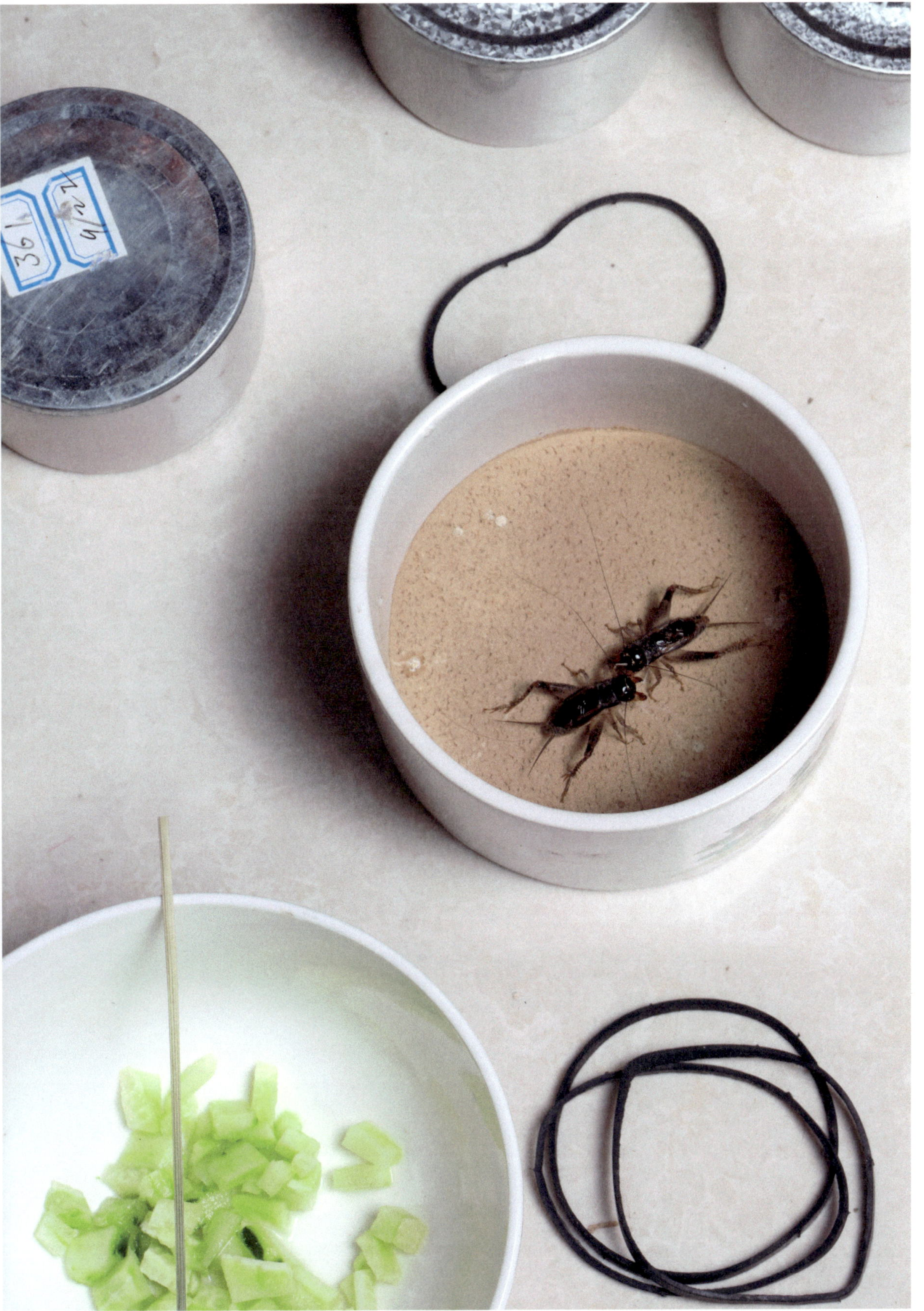

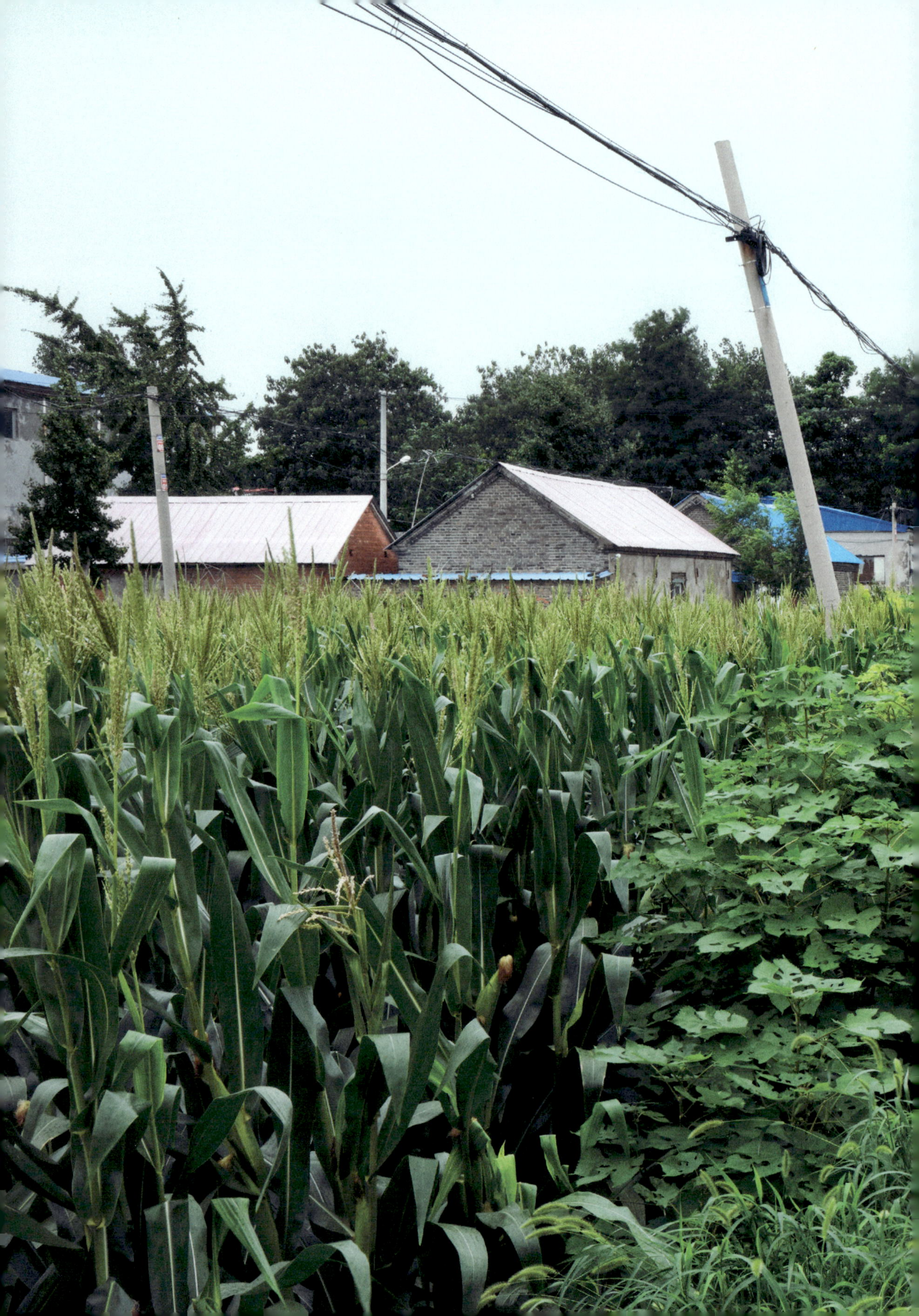

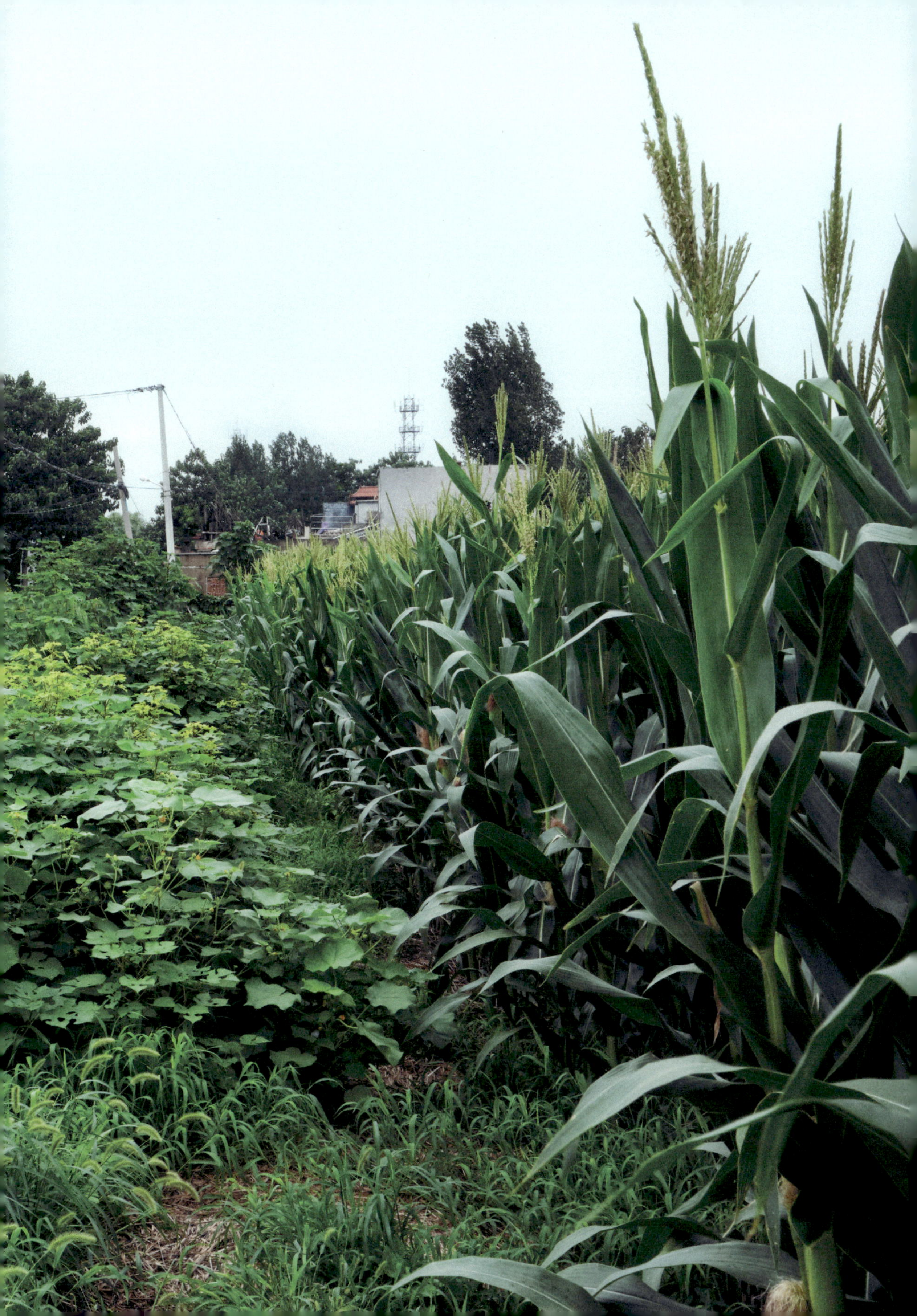

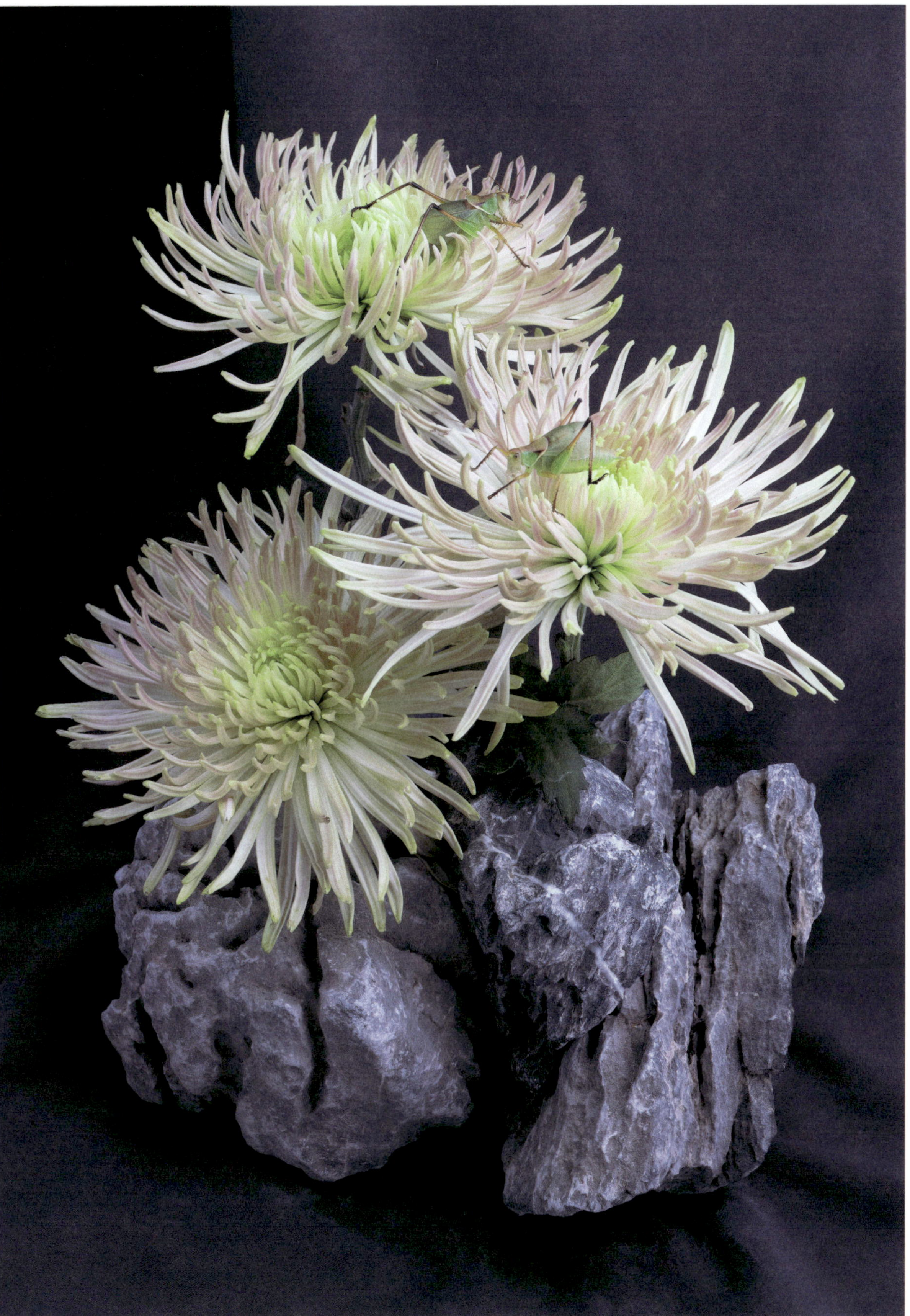

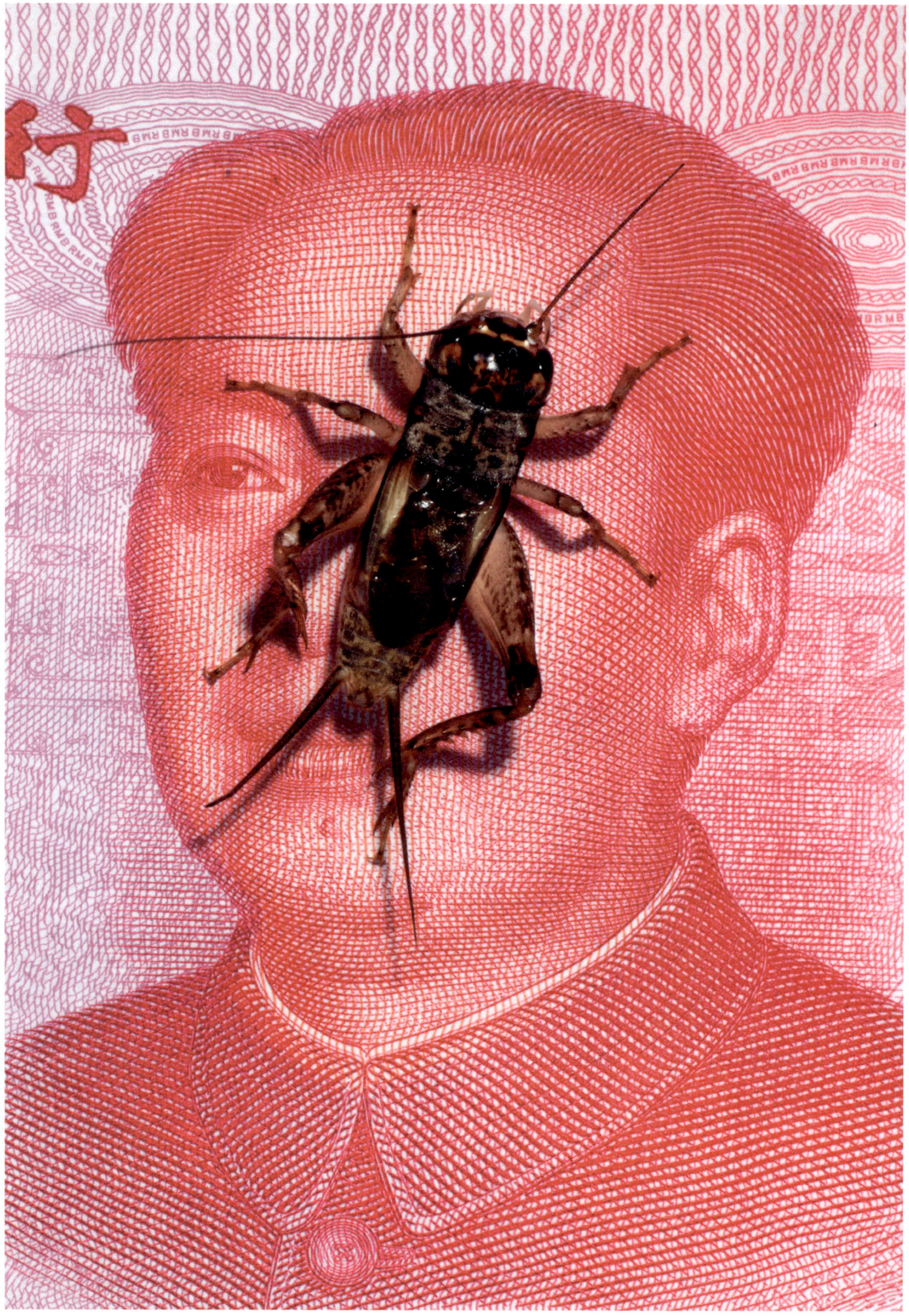

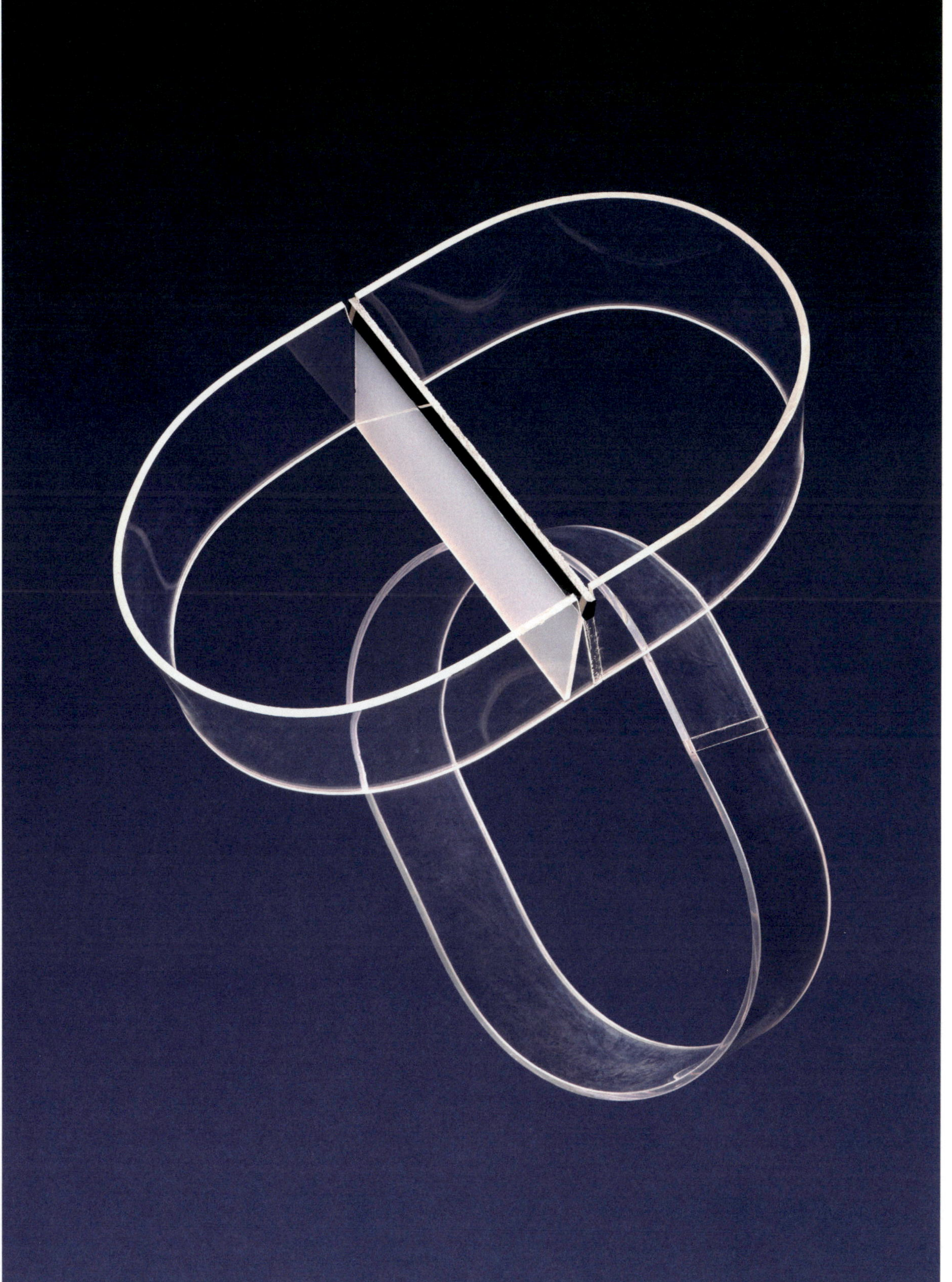

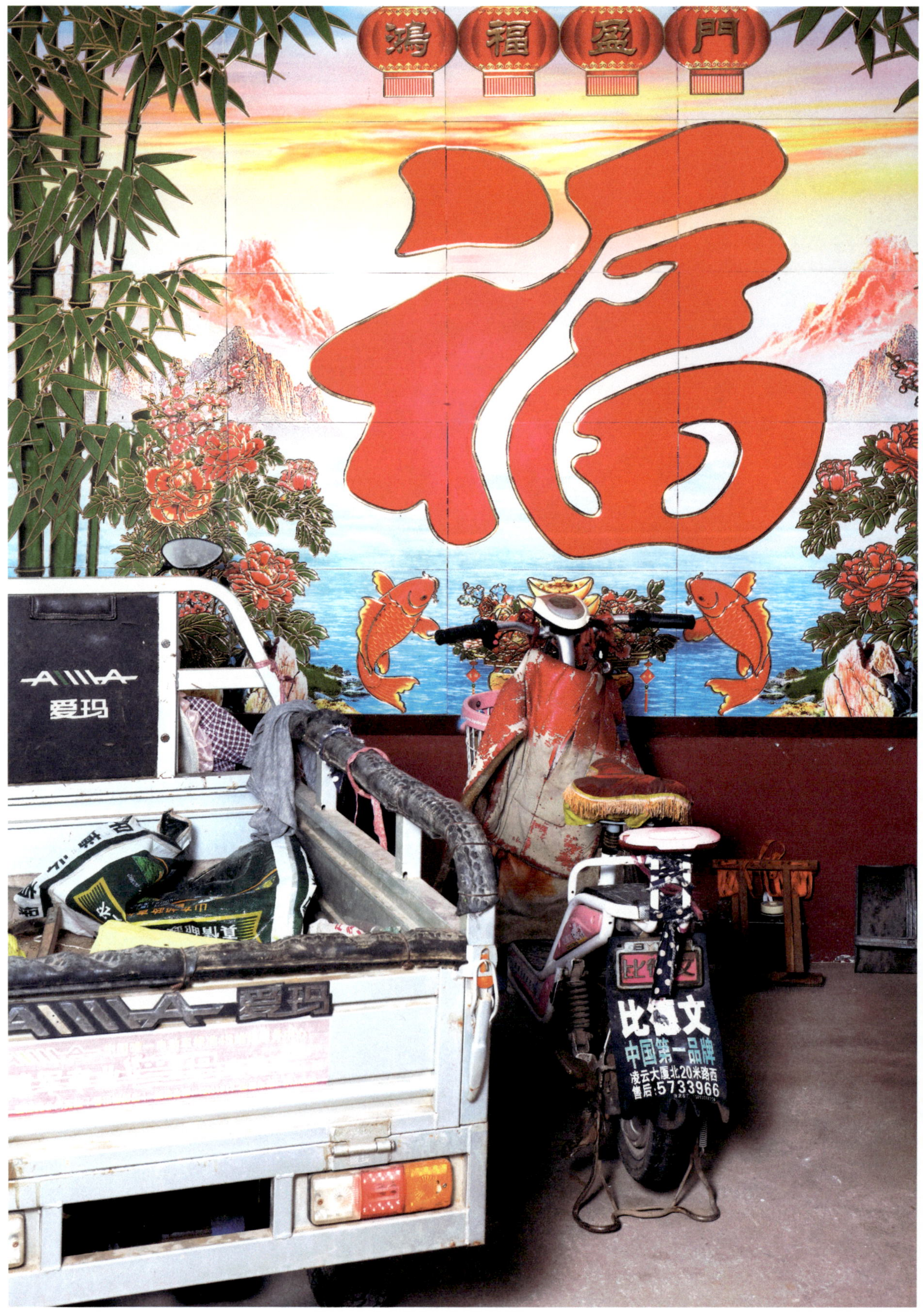
鴻福盈門
福
爱玛
爱玛
中国第一品牌
凌云大厦北20米路西
售后:5733966

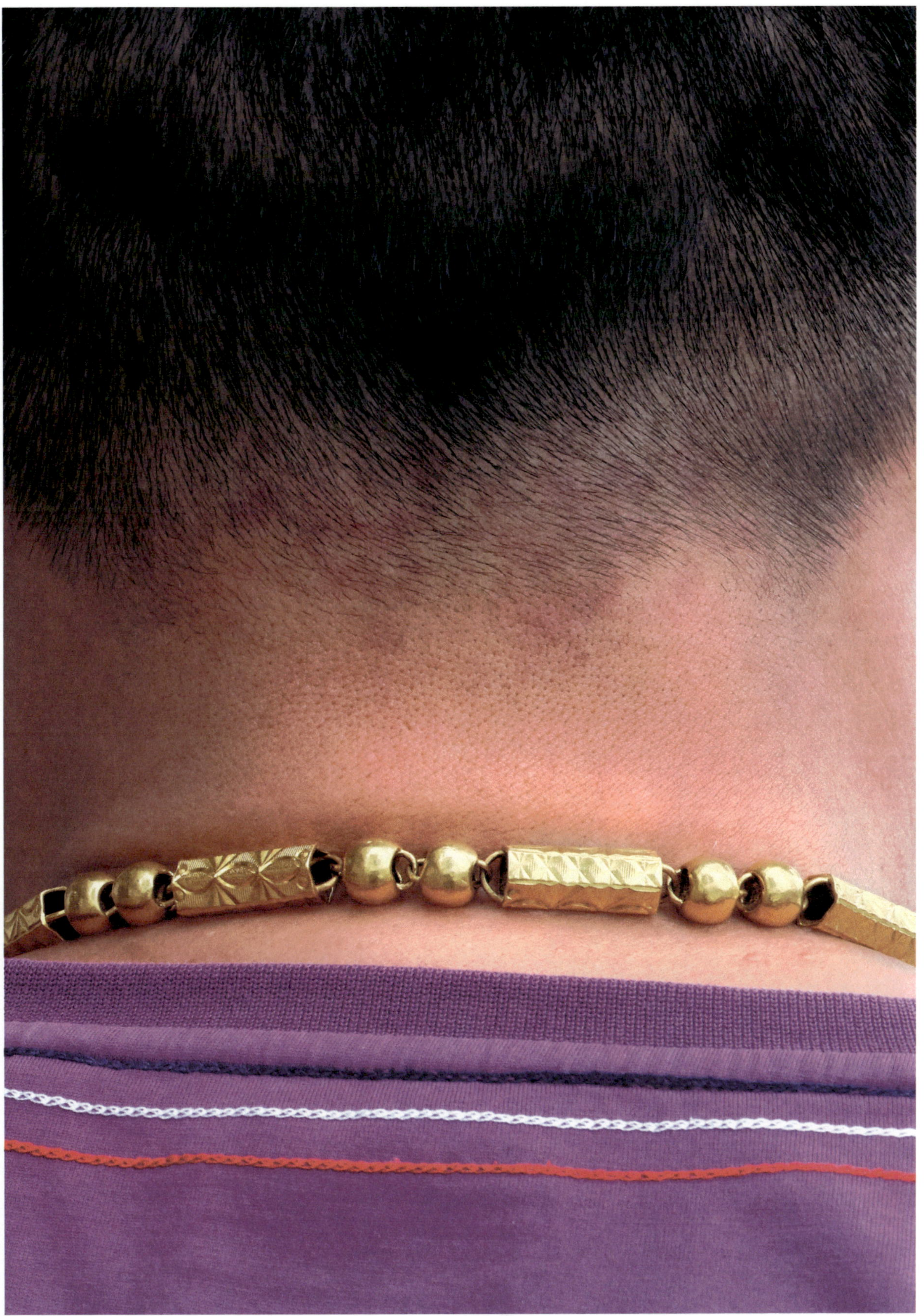

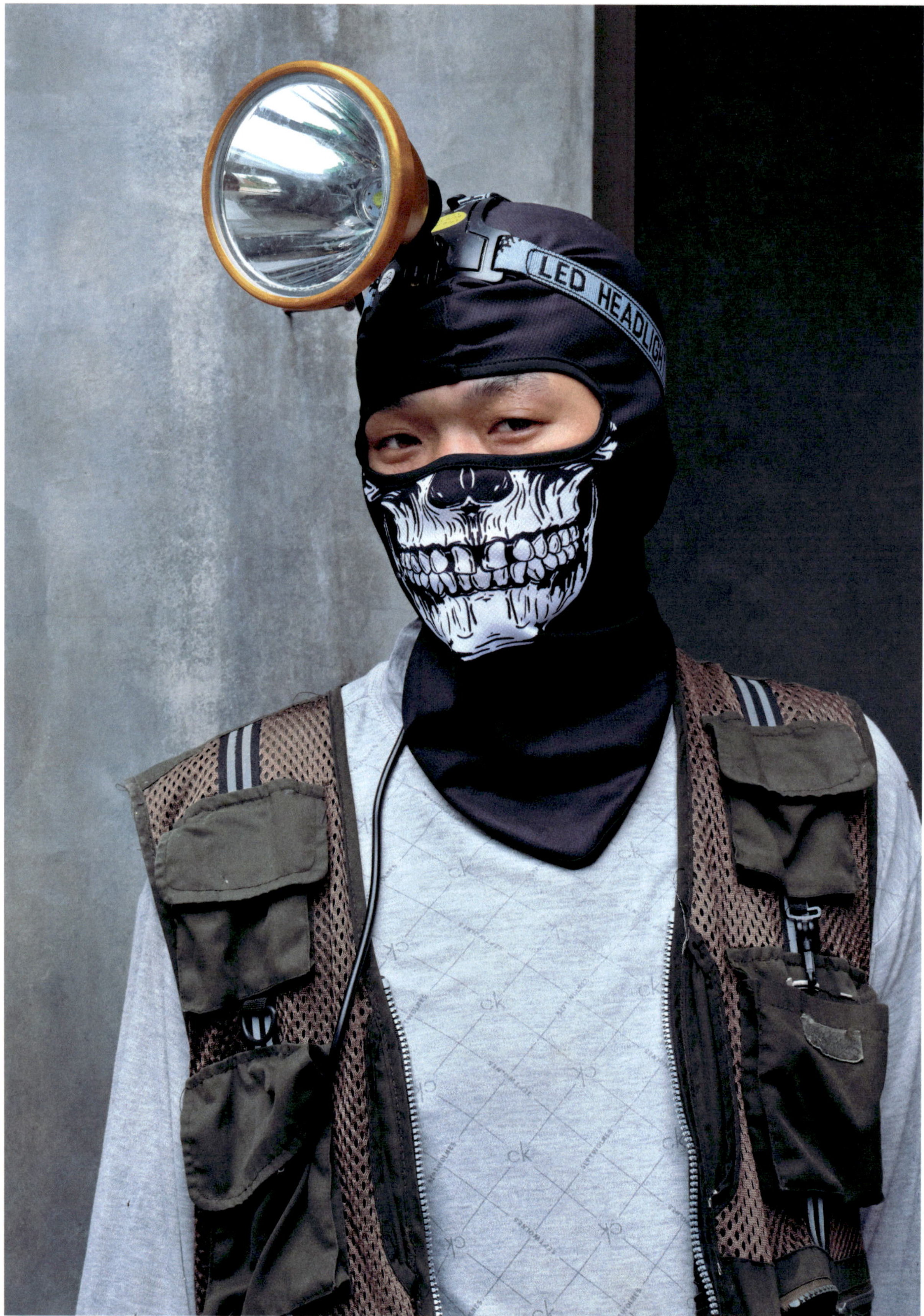
LED

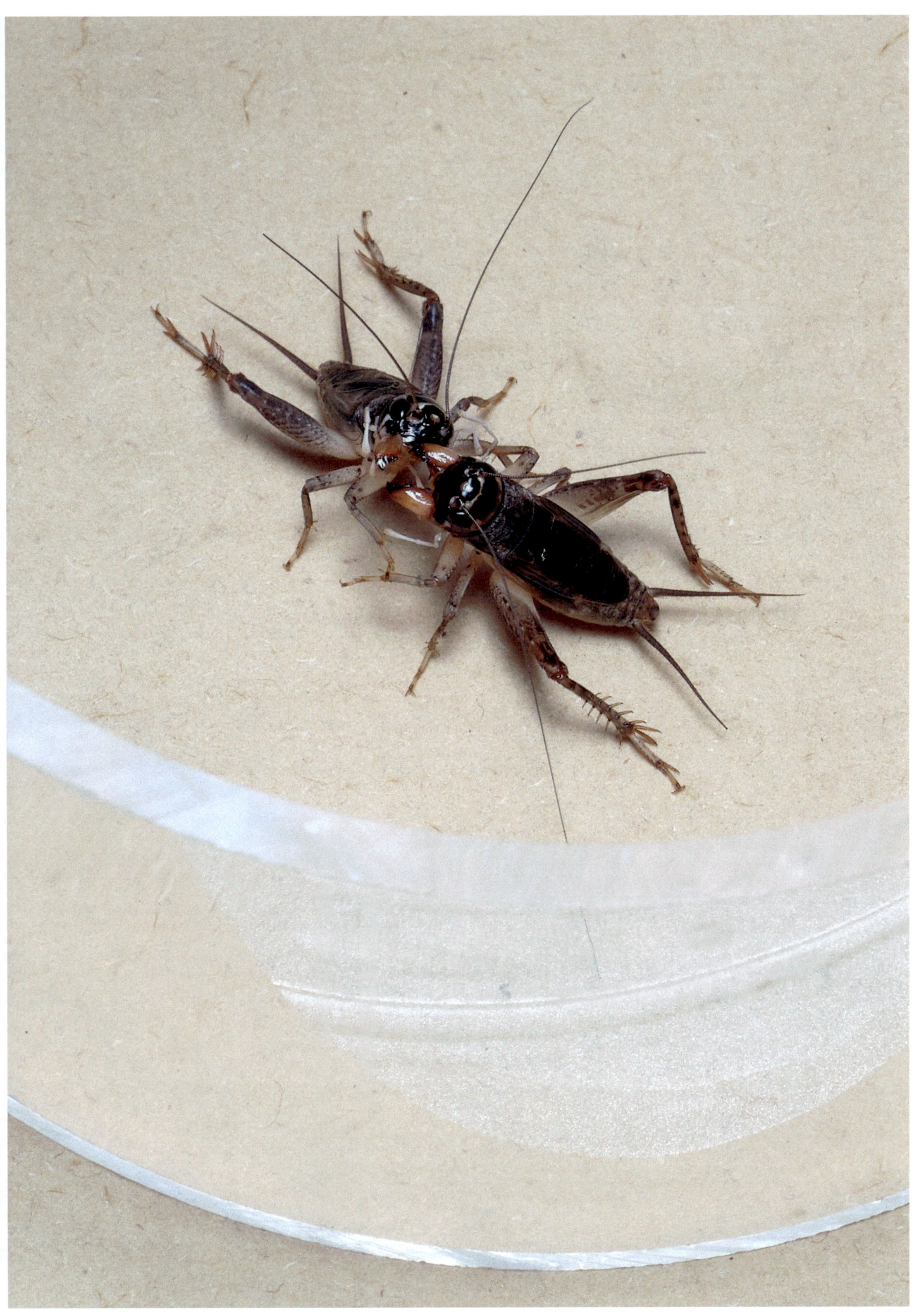

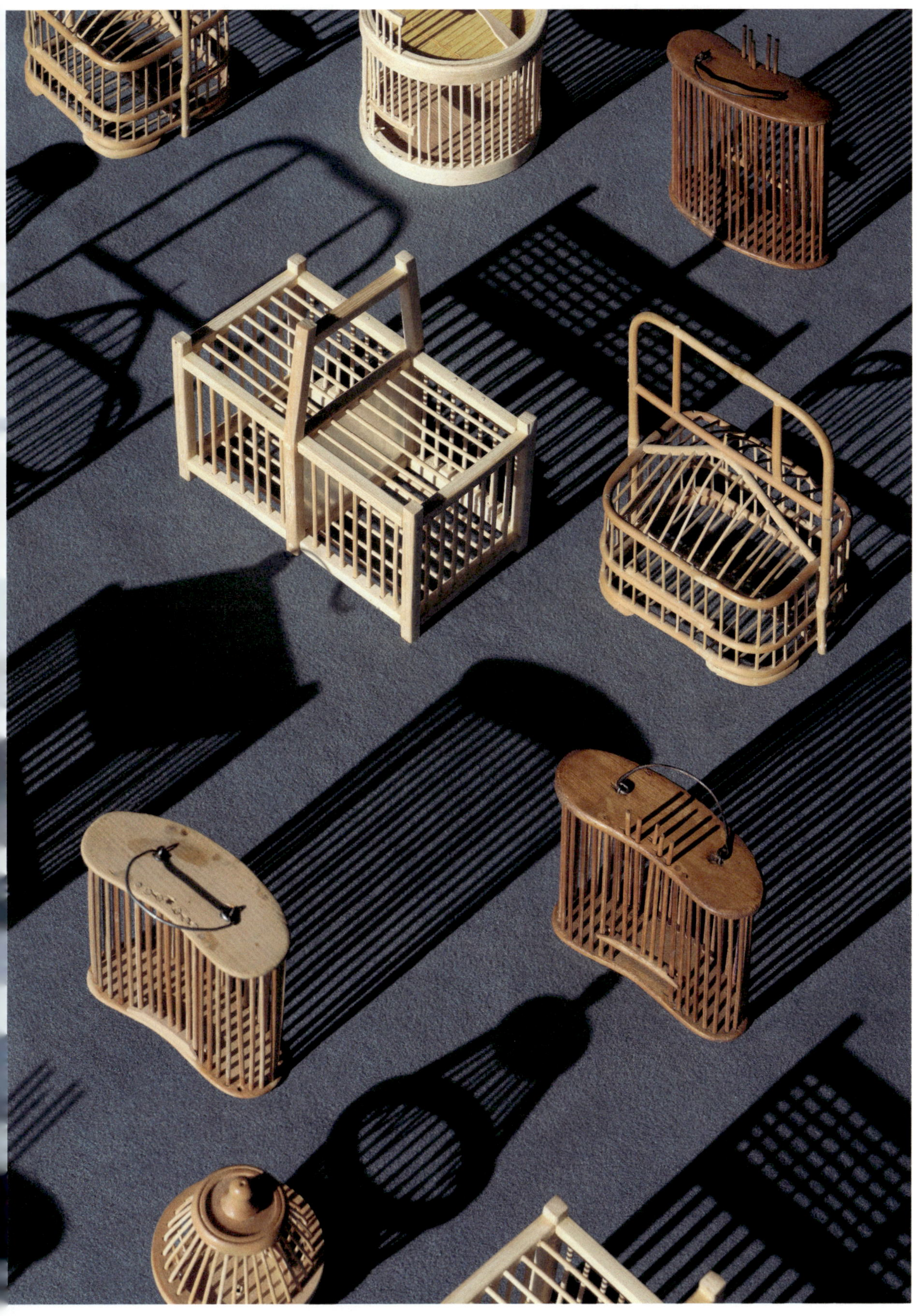

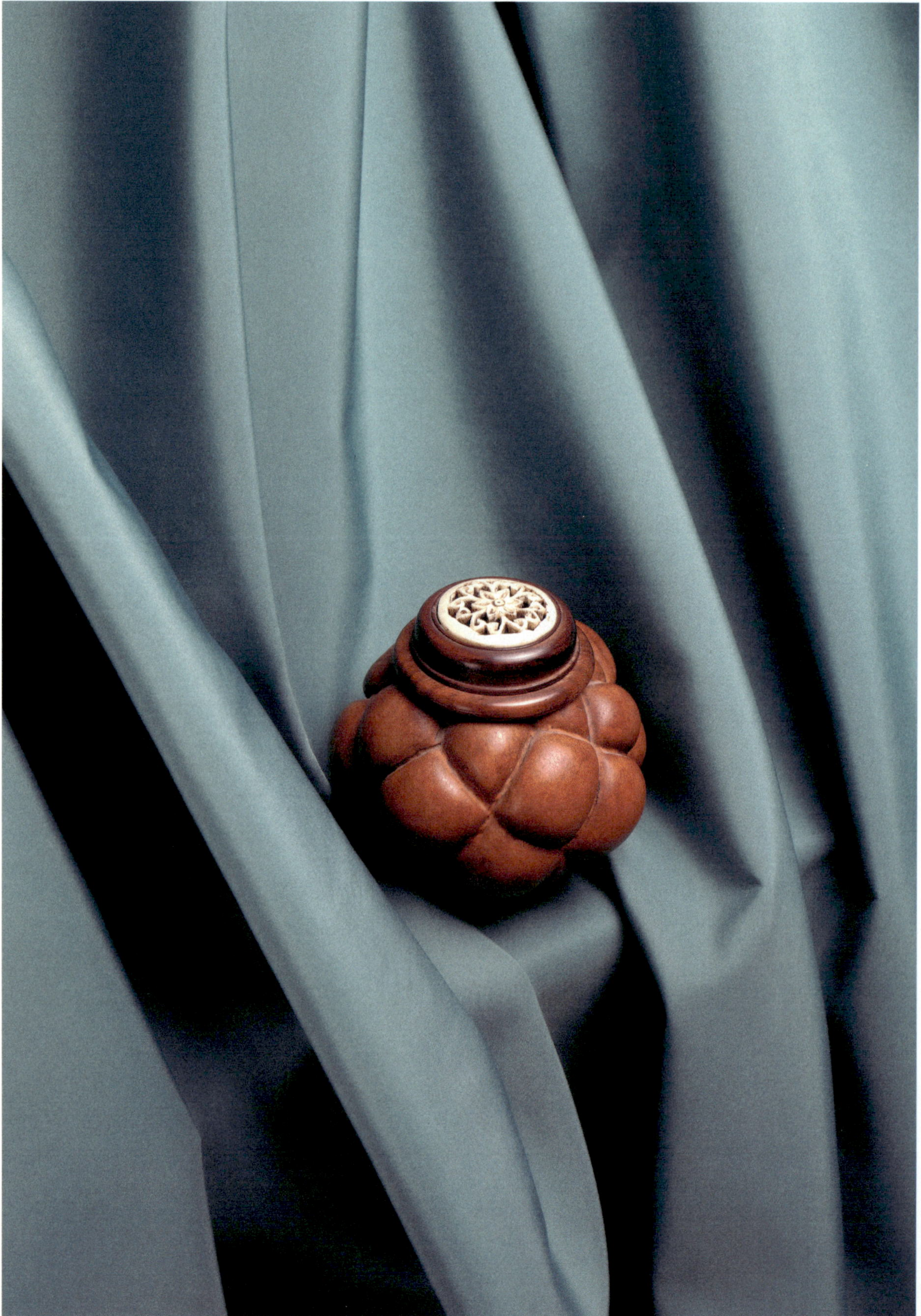

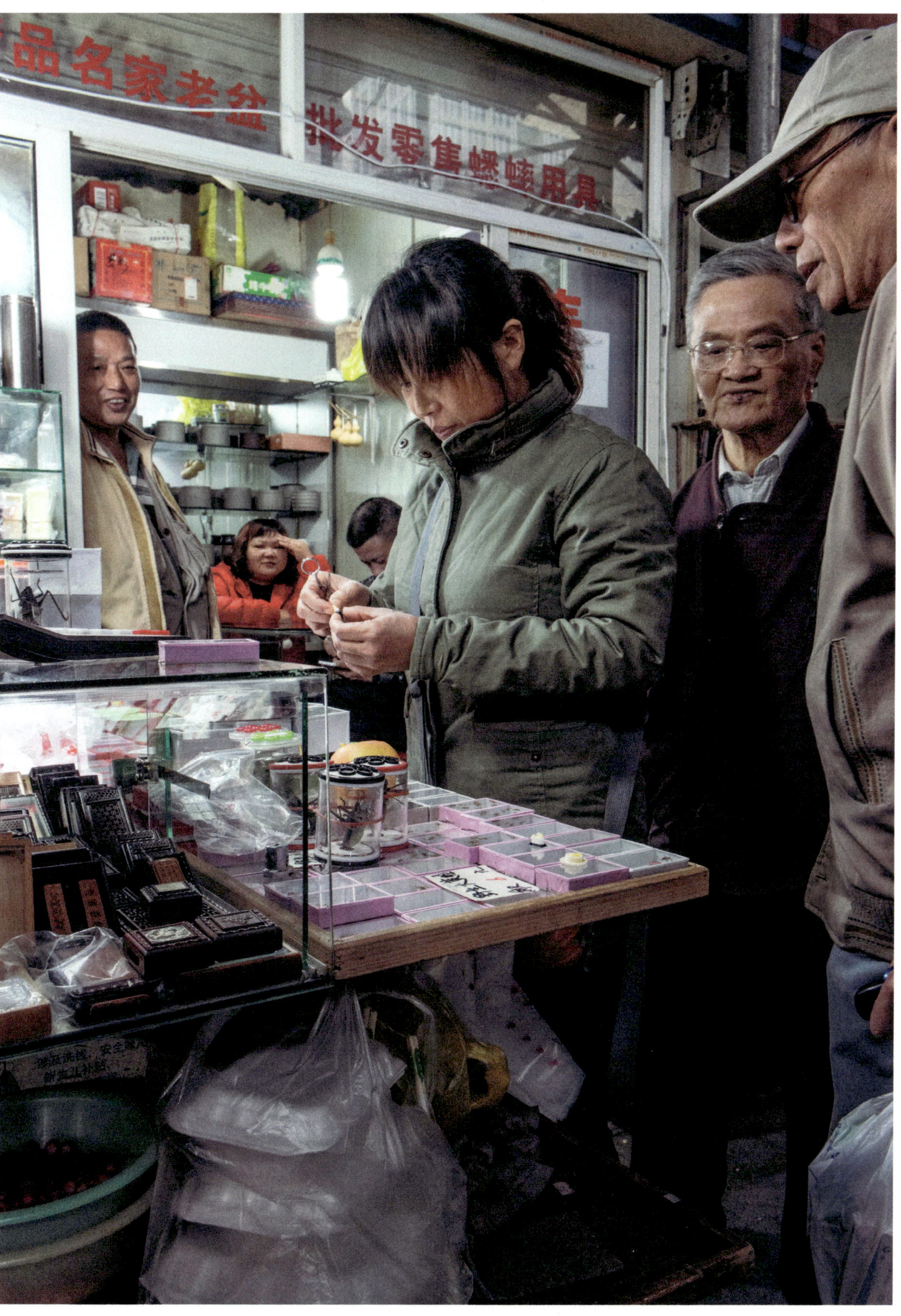
品名家老盆
批发零售蟋蟀用具

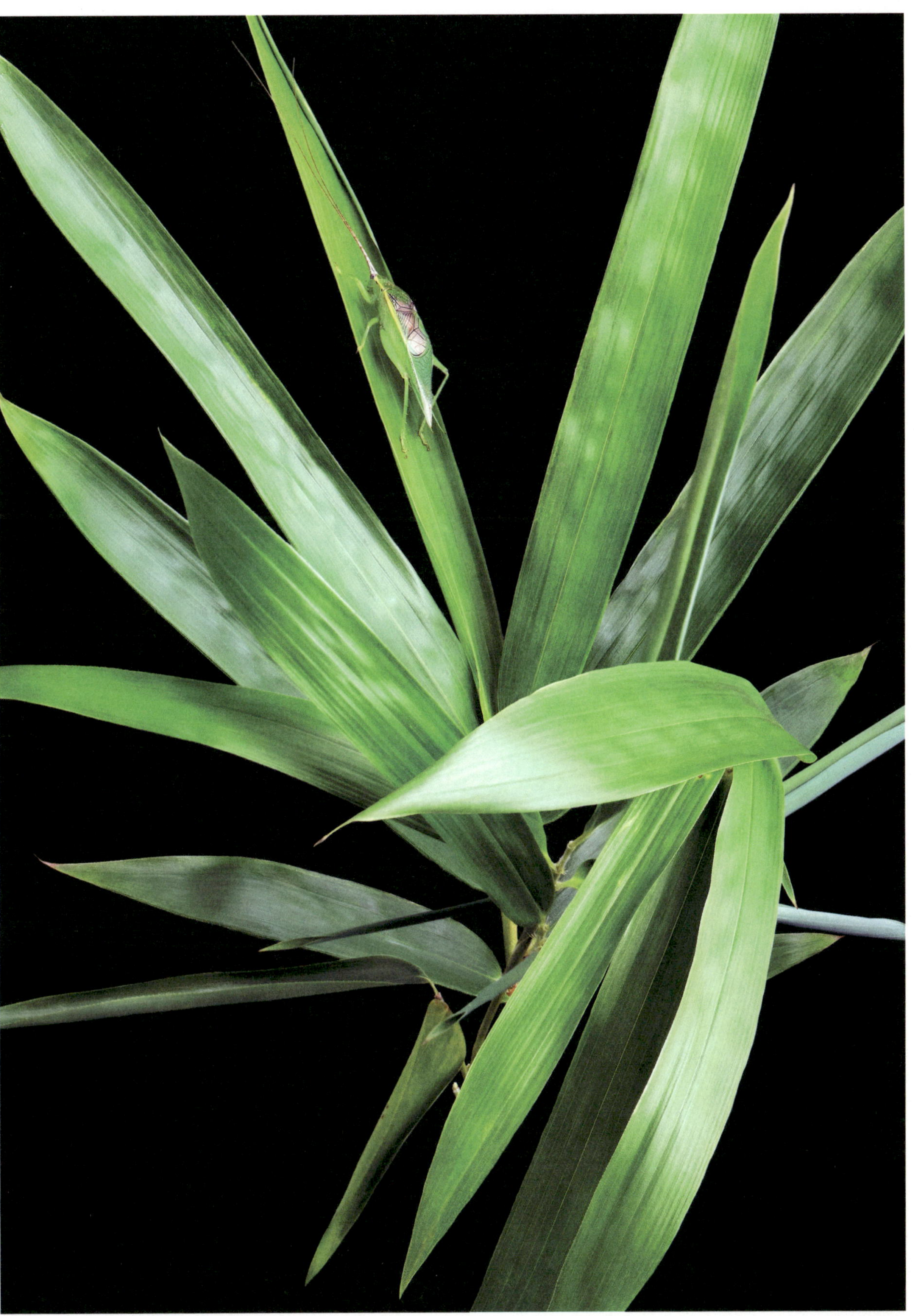

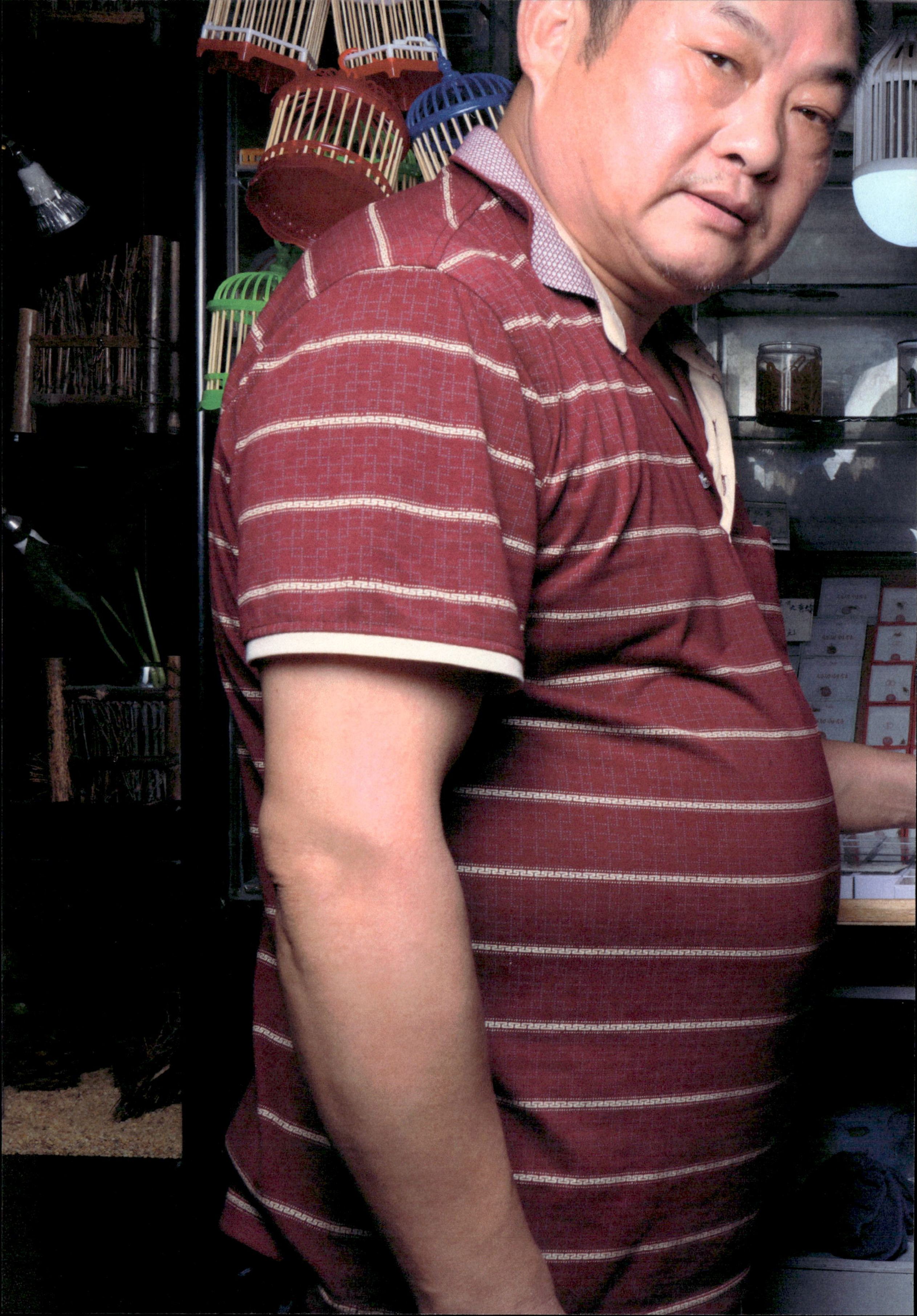

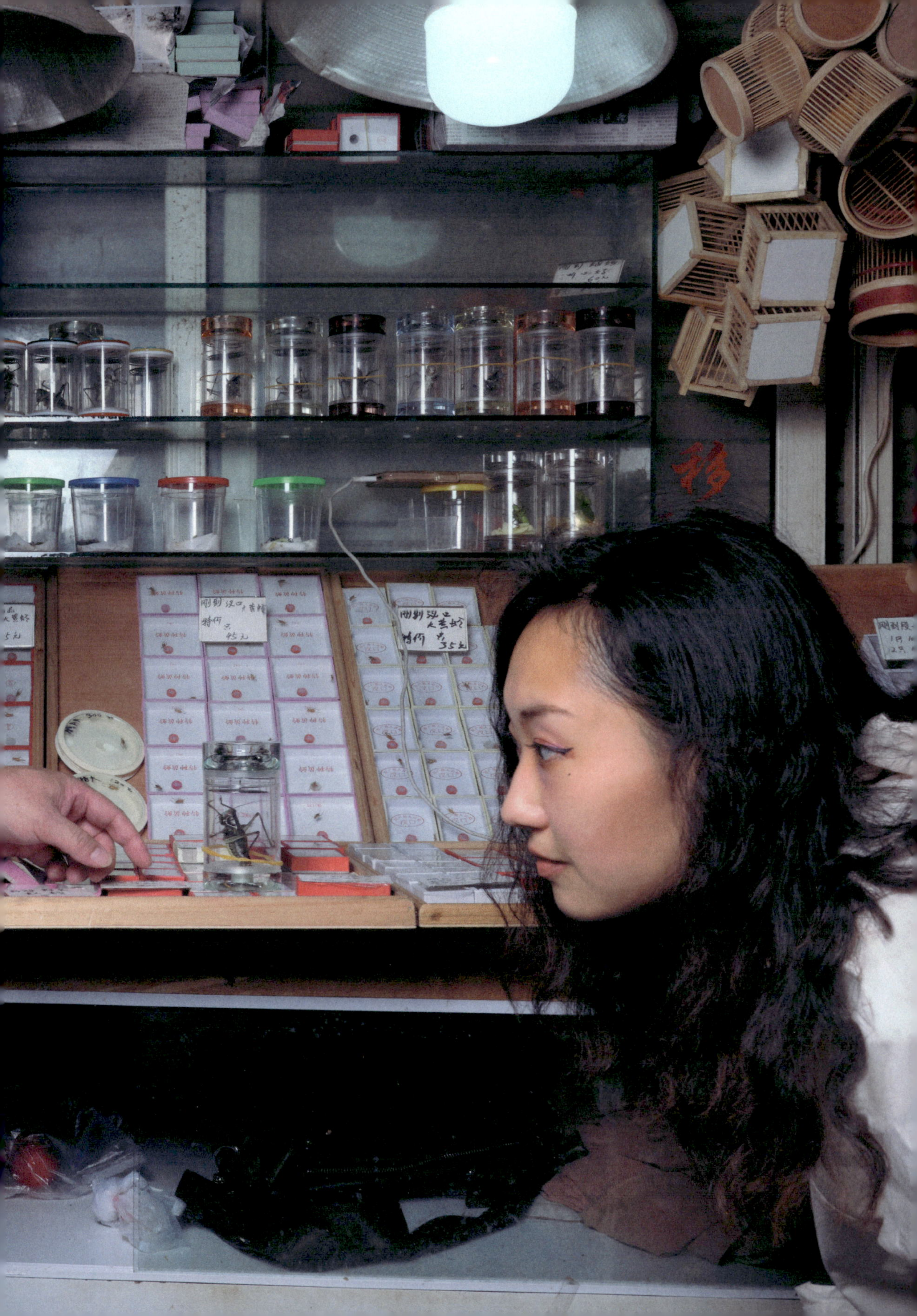
刚到 汉口
特价
45元
刚到 汉口
特价
35元

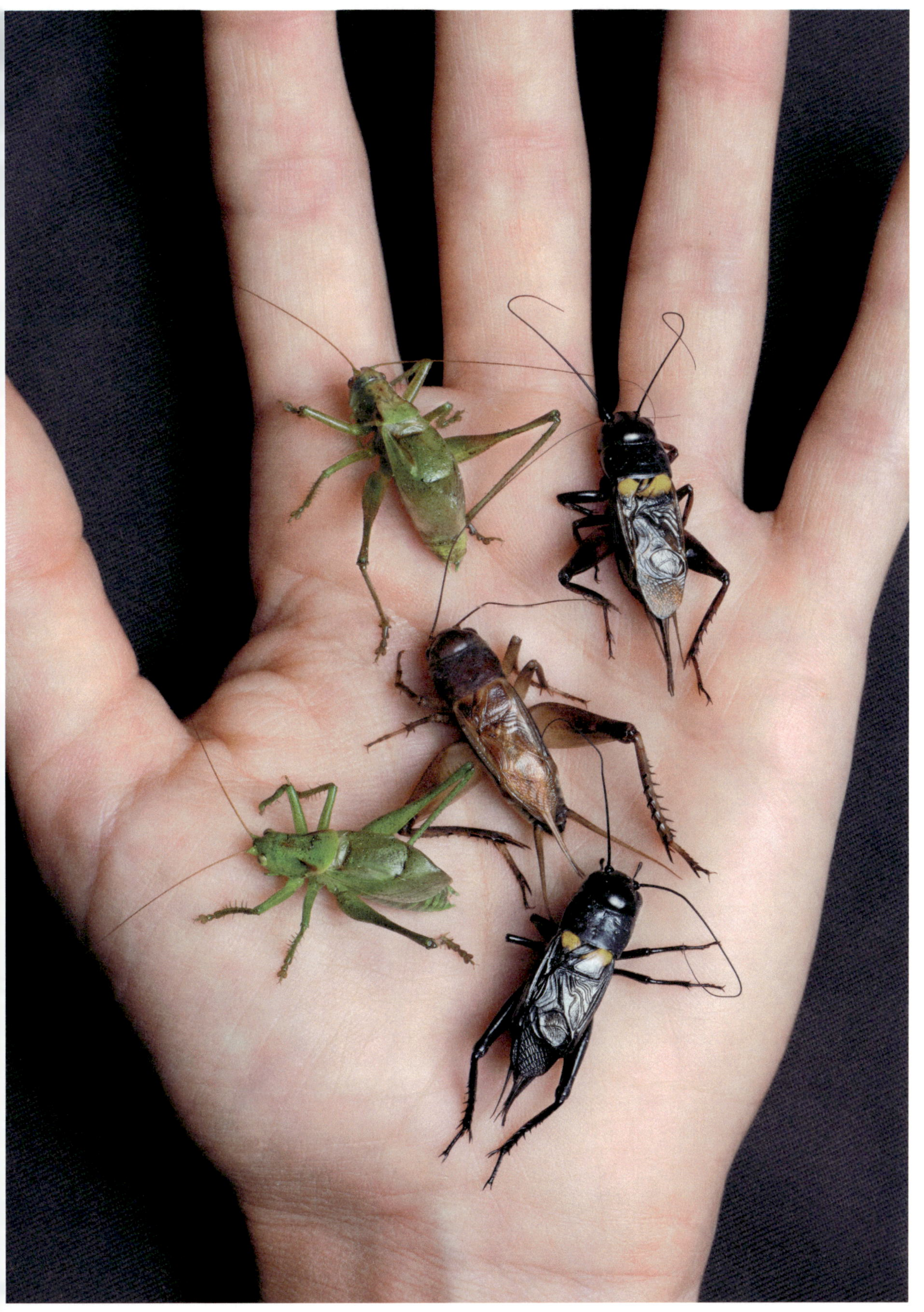

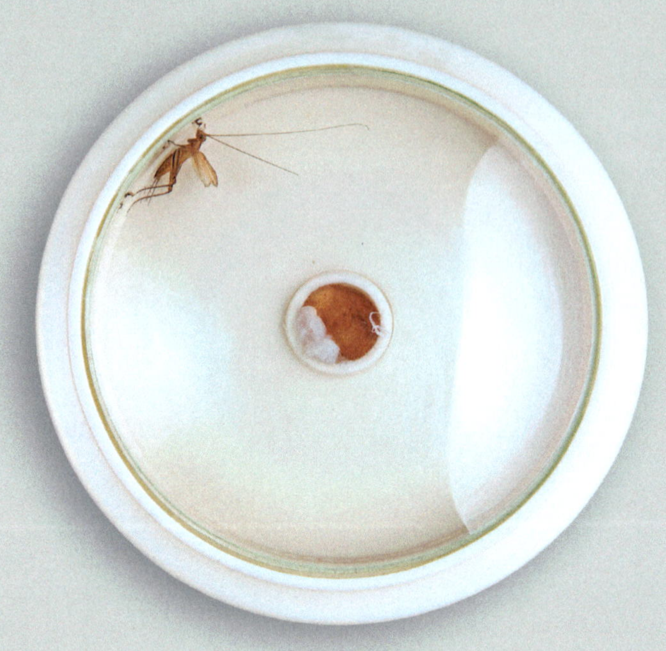

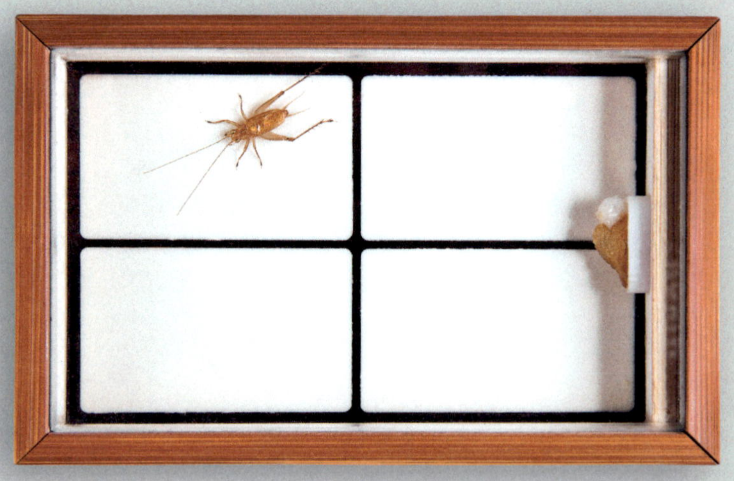

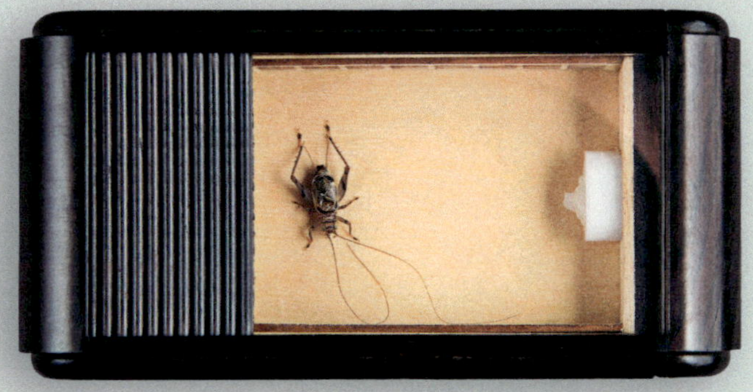

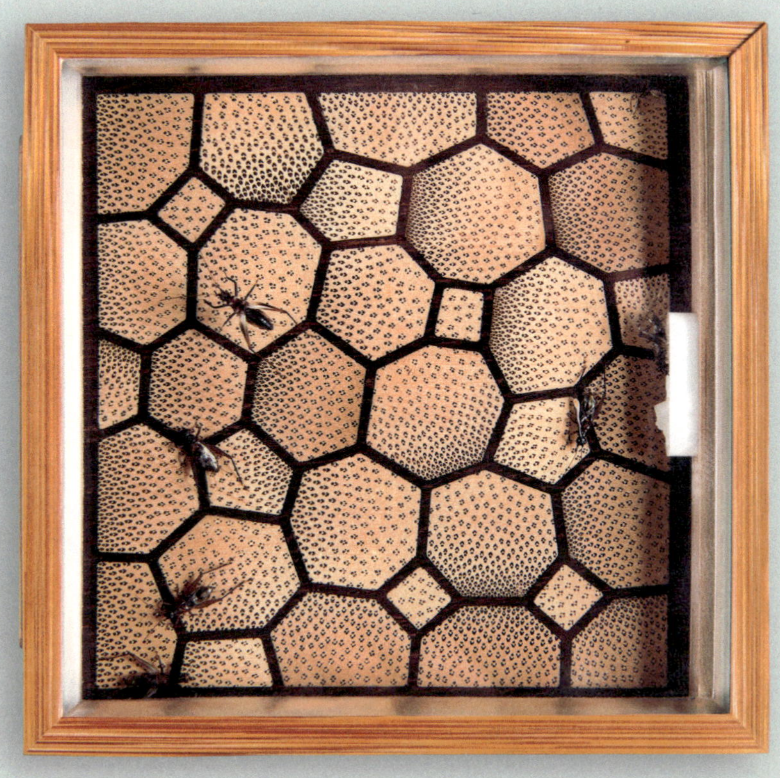

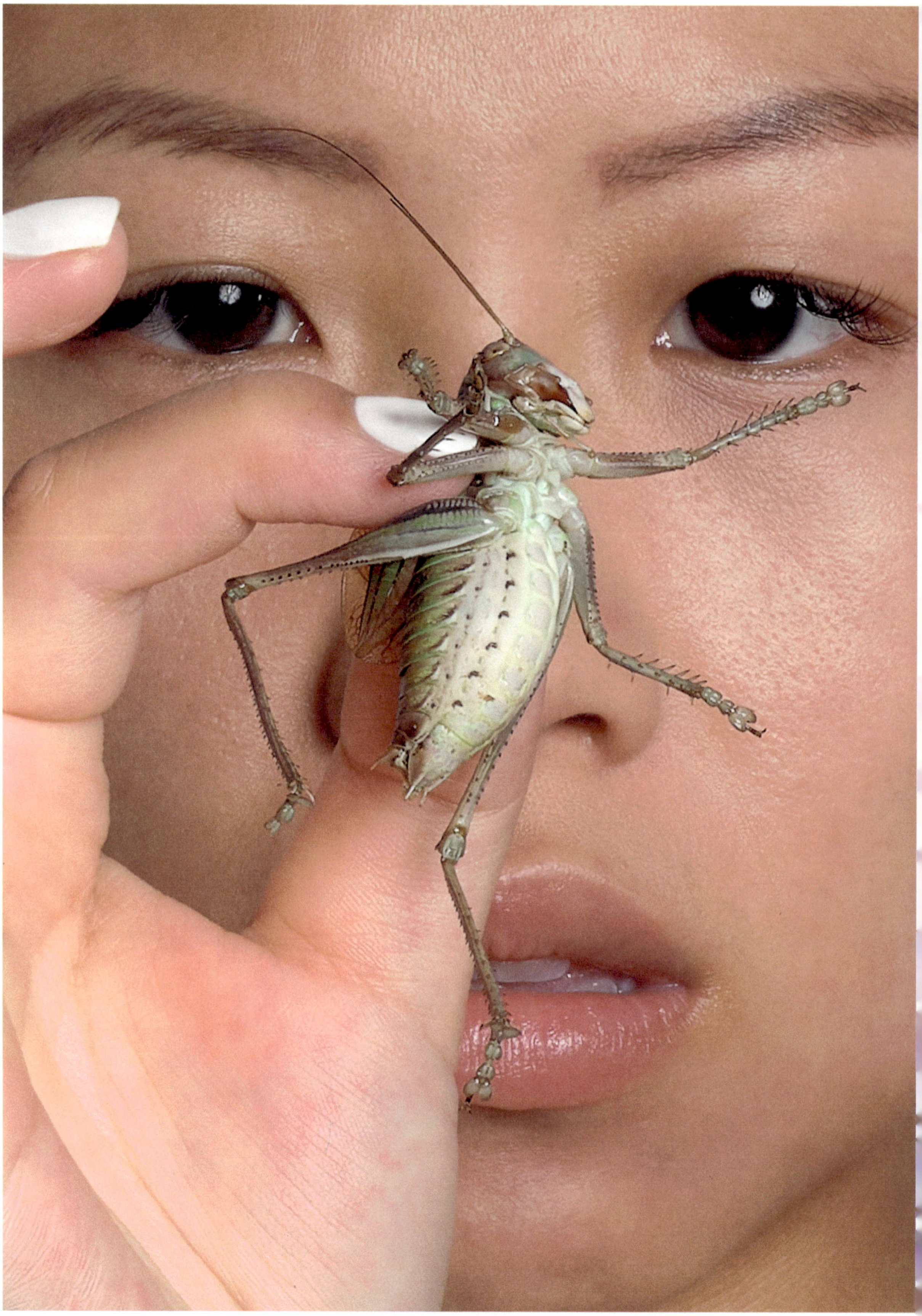

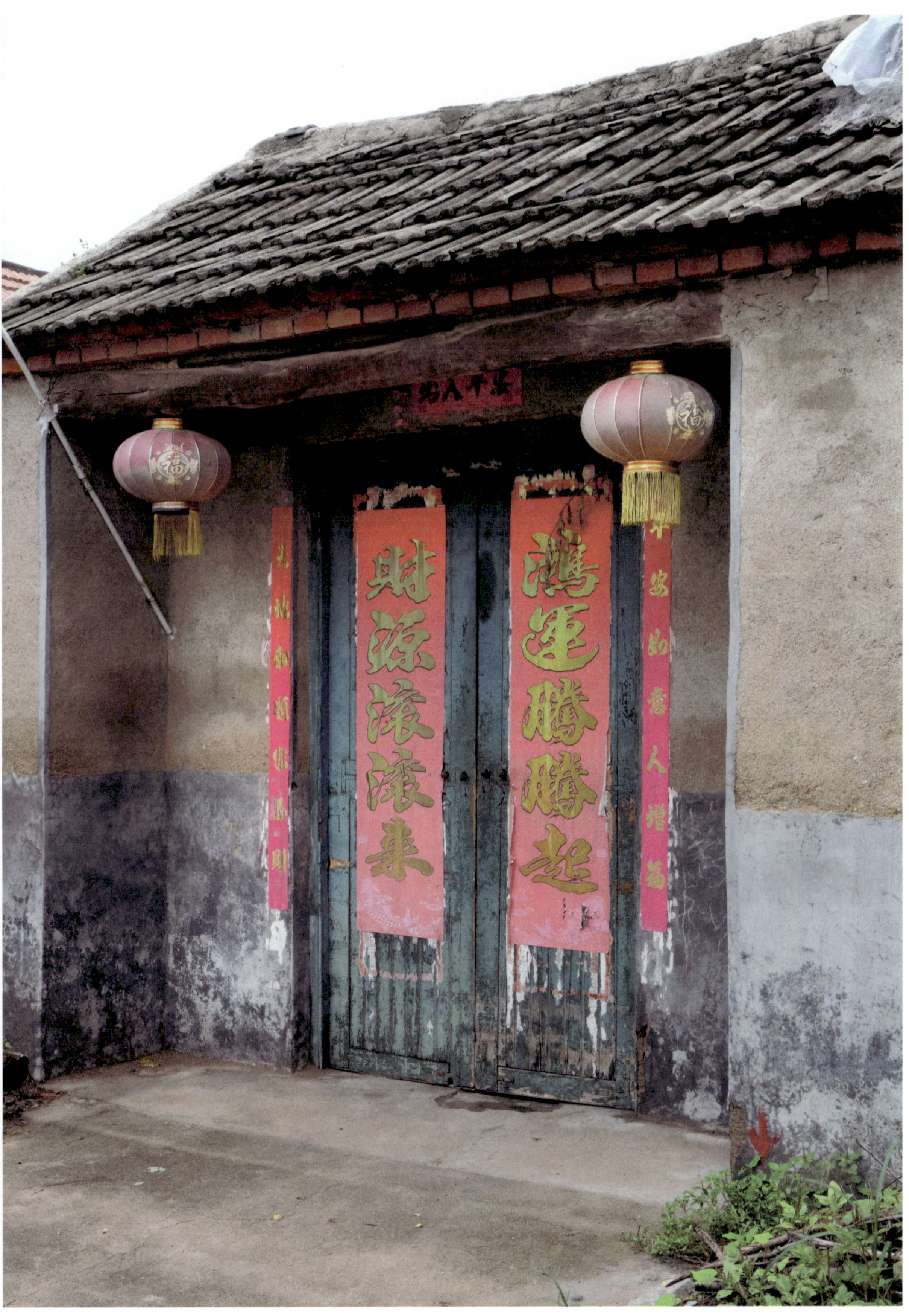
財源滾滾来
鴻運騰騰起

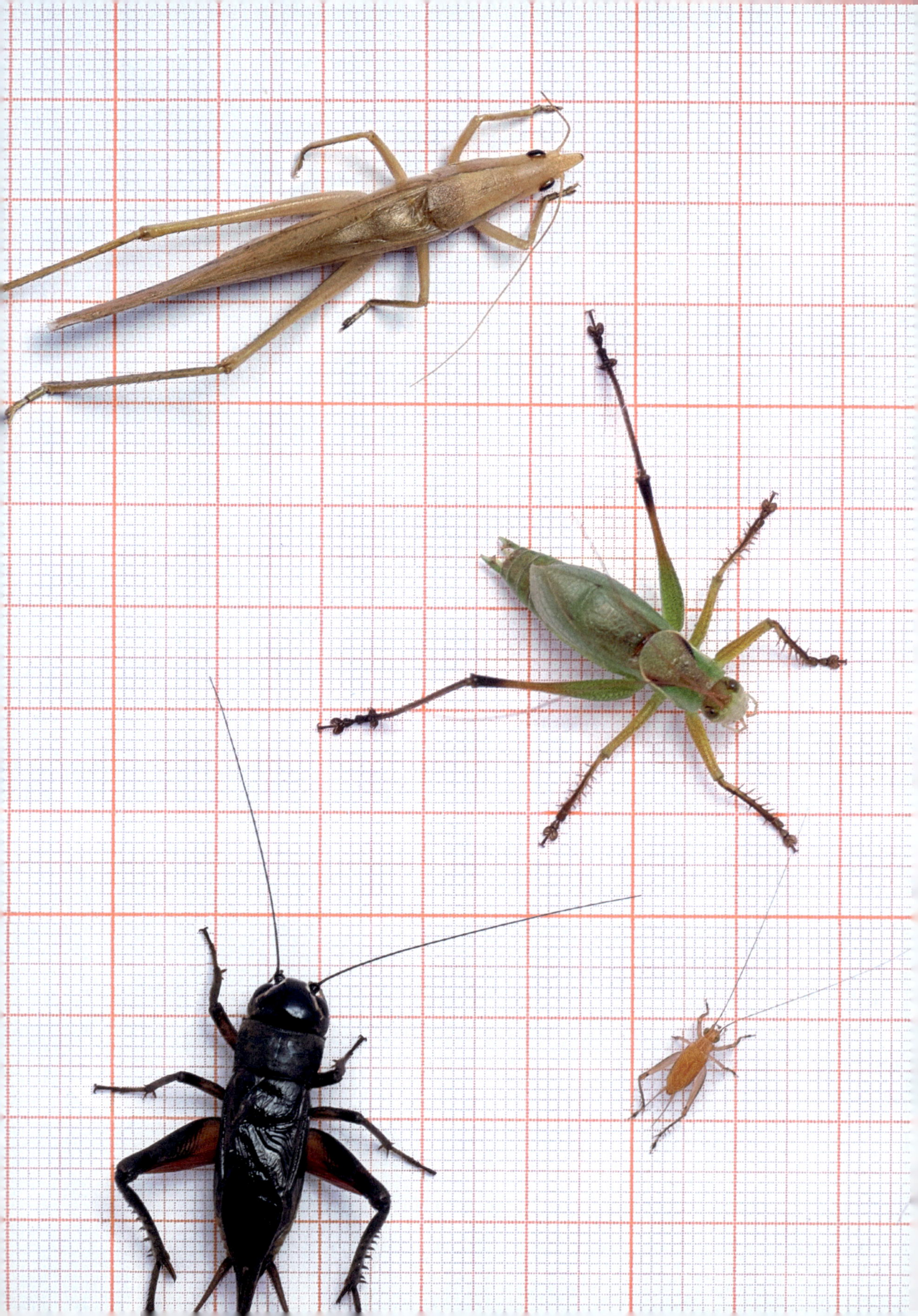

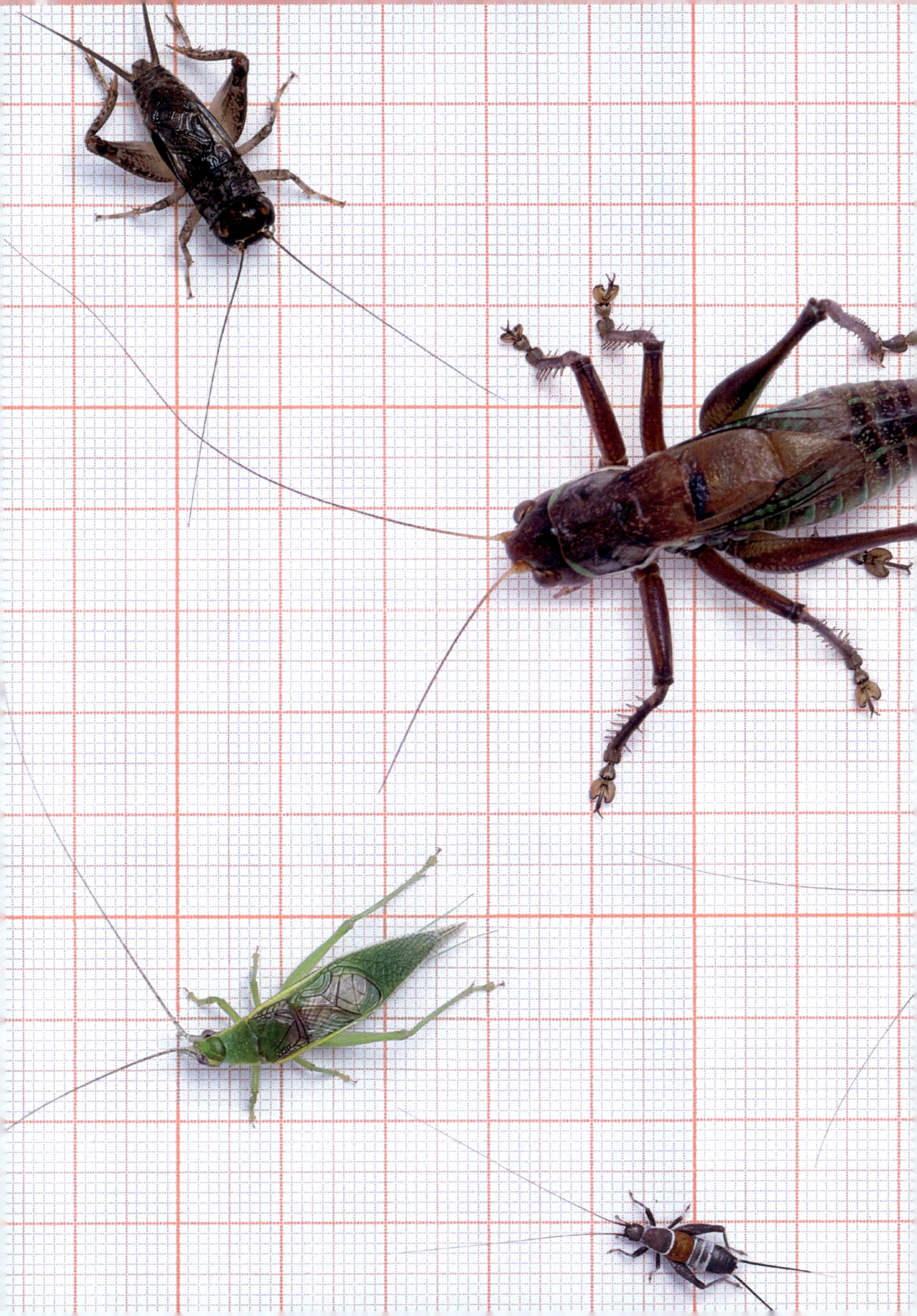

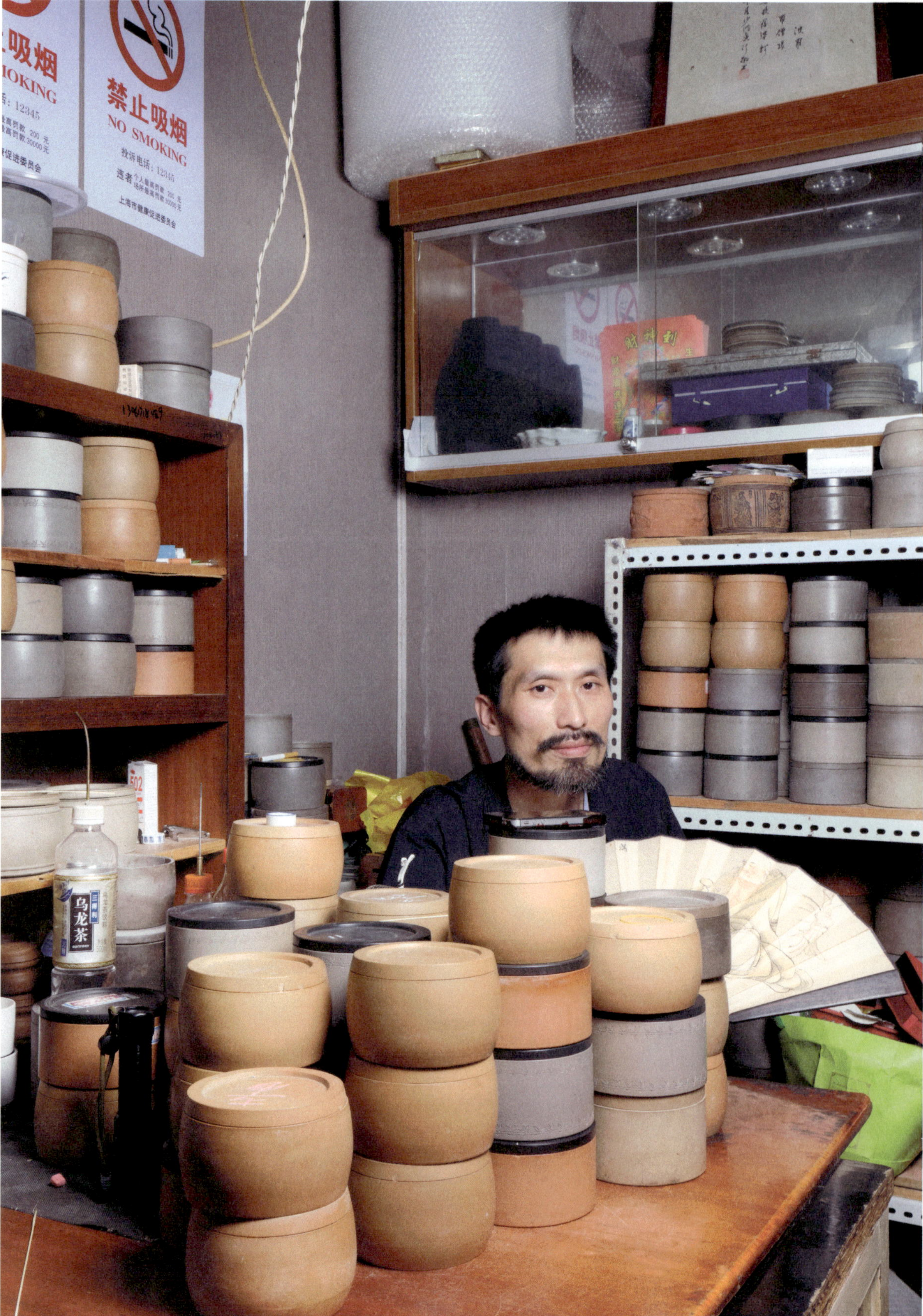

禁止吸烟
NO SMOKING
投诉电话：12345
上海市健康促进委员会
乌龙茶

Laurence Kubski
Crickets
Stories of Chinese Insect Pets

Book Creation
Dino Simonett

Managing Director
Martina Baer

Graphic Design
Dino Simonett and Laurence Kubski

Lithography
Photorotation Geneva

Print
Robstolk Amsterdam

Paper
Munken Print White 115 g

Binding
Boekbinderij Van Waarden Zaandam

Limited Edition of Seven Hundred and Fifty Books

ISBN 978-3-906313-31-3

Simonett & Baer

simonettbaer.com

Laurence Kubski is a Swiss photographer born in 1986. She studied at ECAL/University of Art and Design Lausanne.
Her artistic work is centred on the way people interact with animals in different cultures.

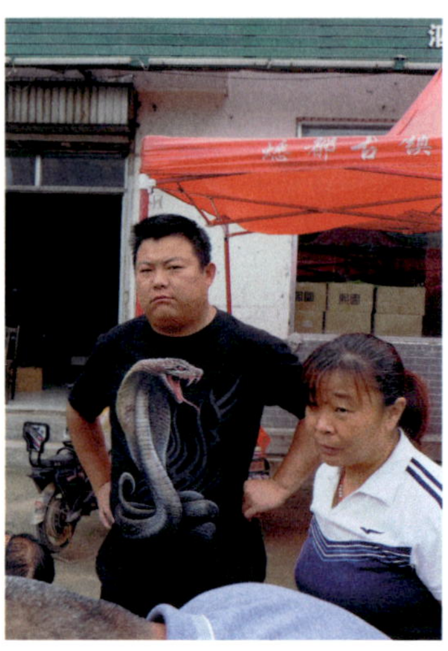

With special thanks to: Martina Baer, Sandro Bolzoni, Hong Chao, Junyan Cheng, Shen Chun, Philippe Egger, Pierre Fantys, Erwan Frotin, Alexis Georgacopoulos, Dominique Gex, Florence Graezer Bideau, Julien Gremaud, Helen Ho, Sheena Kennedy, Christiane, Grégoire, Marc André, Thomas and Xavier Kubski, Han Li, Jing Liang, Family Lu, Jessica Mantel, Luc Meier, Han Minying, Caroline Nicod, Anne-Sophie Panow, Augustin Scott de Martinville, Laurent Scott de Martinville, Dino Simonett, Marinie Tao, Anne Thiollier, vfg Nachwuchsförderpreis für Fotografie team, Wen Xiang Shi, Sophie Xue, Qianqian Zhang, Yue Zhang.

prohelvetia

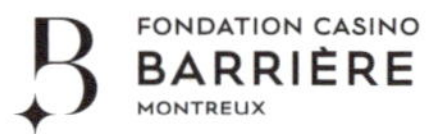

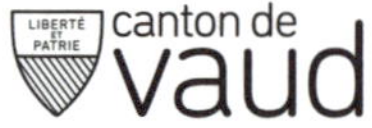

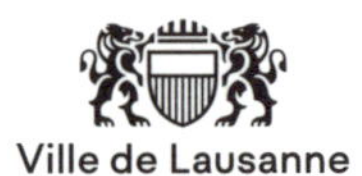

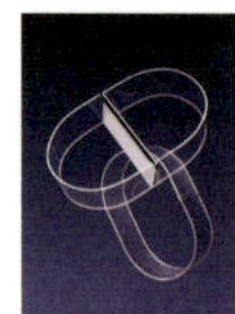
Transparent arenas for cricket fights, with a removable divider.

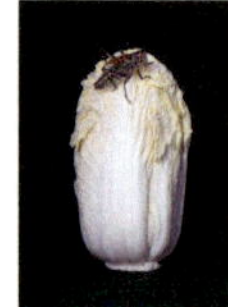
Bush crickets are traditionally represented with cabbage in Chinese art.

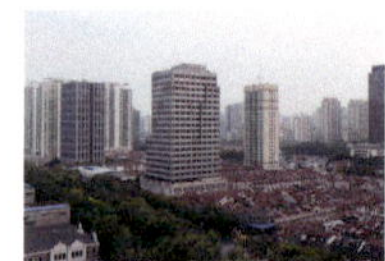
Wan Shang market in Shanghai, the largest insect market in China.

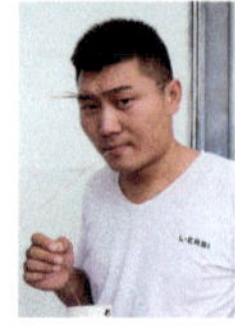
Trader testing a cricket's aggressiveness and combat skills.

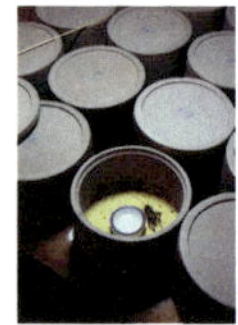
Each cricket must be kept in its own clay pot.

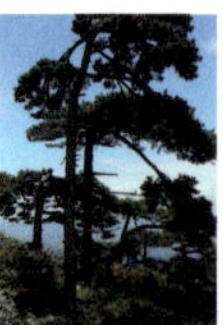
Northeastern Shandong Province's climate produces a particularly fierce breed.

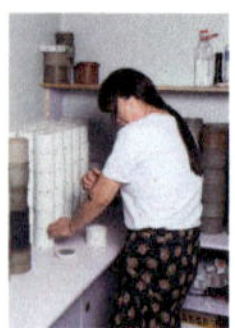
Wan Shang market trader feeding fighting crickets.

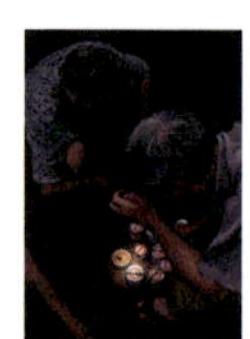
Fighting aficionados looking to buy a new champion.

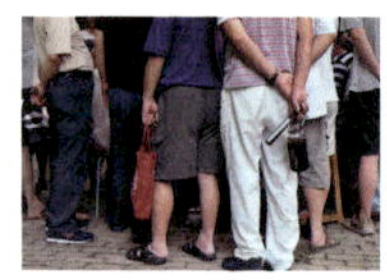
Retired men watching cricket fights in a park.

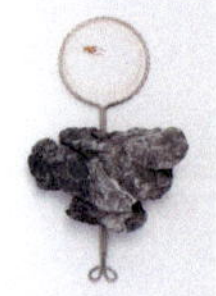
Specimen of small singing cricket.

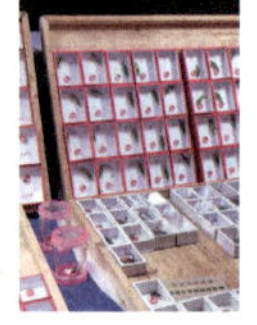
Display of singers in Wan Shang market.

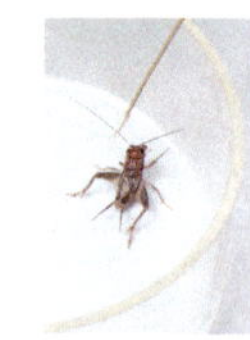
Stirring a fighter into action before the match.

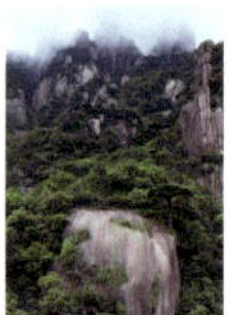
Insects play a crucial role as indicators of seasonal changes.

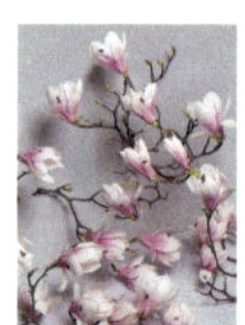
Spring composition with magnolias.

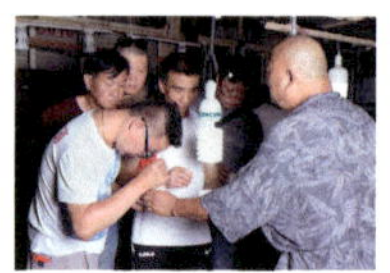
Buyer testing a fighter surrounded by potential rivals.

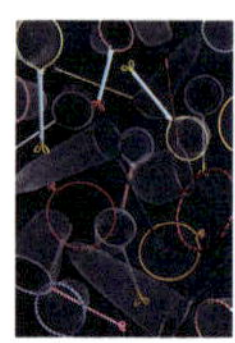
Nets specifically designed for catching crickets.

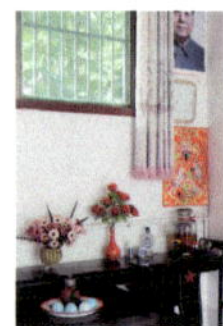
Lu family living room with pictures of Mao and the god of fortune.

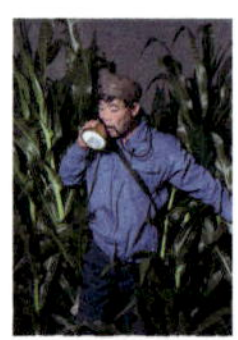
Men catch crickets at night.

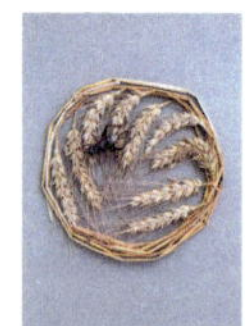
Traditional pattern of nine ears of wheat.

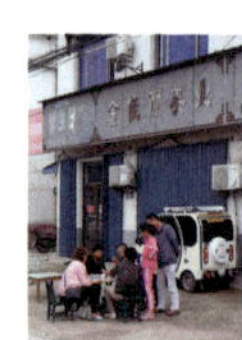
Trader in Sidian who rent a space with a small table on the sidewalk.

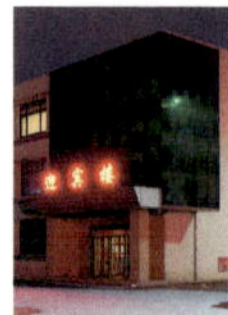
Hotels near Sidian resonate in summer with the chirping of insects.

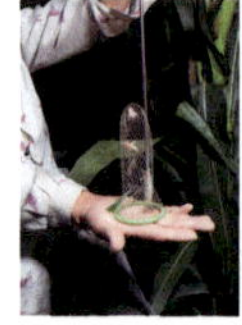
The capture equipment is simple: a flashlight, a net and a container.

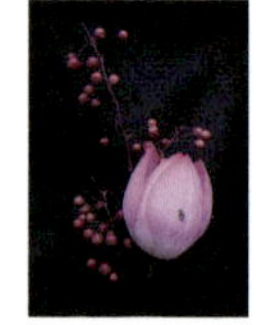
Summer composition with lotus.

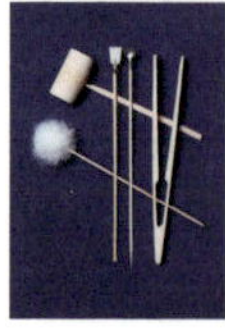
Tools to feed, groom and handle the crickets during fights.